The Alien Princess Diaries

The Alien Princess Diaries

The Paranormal Story of a
Recovering Addict

Daniel Fritz

Copyright © 2011 by Daniel Fritz.

Library of Congress Control Number: 2011914723
ISBN: Hardcover   978-1-4653-5234-7
              Softcover   978-1-4653-5233-0
              Ebook   978-1-4653-5235-4

All rights reserved. No part of this book may be reproduced or transmitted in any form or by any means, electronic or mechanical, including photocopying, recording, or by any information storage and retrieval system, without permission in writing from the copyright owner.

This book was printed in the United States of America.

To order additional copies of this book, contact:
Xlibris Corporation
1-888-795-4274
www.Xlibris.com
Orders@Xlibris.com
103792

Contents

Foreword 9
Prologue 11
  1. God, Grant Us the Serenity 17
  2. I'm Your Venus 23
  3. A Rough Beginning 31
  4. The Building Calls Me Back 40
  5. Naked Neighbors 46
  6. Trouble on the Streets 54
  7. Universal Blossom? 57
  8. Boys Will Be Boys 62
  9. My Christmas Gift 69
10. Jake the Snake? 74
11. Angels and Aliens 81
12. The Inquisition 85
13. Nothing to Fear 88
14. Catch and Release 92
15. Smile, Playboy, You're on TV 96
16. Vanity is Insanity 101
17. Love is the Answer 106
18. Sweet Dream or Beautiful Nightmare? 110
19. Full Circle 116

Dedication

This book is dedicated to my loving brother, who has always been there to carry me.

I would also like to thank Lauren Acevedo and her family, as well as the wonderful staff at Highland Rivers in Rome, GA for creating a space for me to write this book.

Author's Foreword

The following is a true story. While it is based on actual events, parts of the story are meant to take you inside the wildly imaginative mind of a meth addict. Recreational drugs of any kind are often taken as a form of escapism. One of crystal meth's most seductive qualities is its tendency to blur the lines between fantasy and reality. This may lead the user to question what "reality" means in the first place. This can actually be an important question for anyone to ponder. In this world, things are not often what they appear to be. You be the judge.

The names have been changed to protect the innocent (and the not-so-innocent!). Welcome to my crazy world.

Prologue

"The tumors appear to be shrinking." I could barely believe my ears.

"Seriously?" I asked the doctor incredulously. It was the first piece of promising news that we had been given since Grant's initial diagnosis almost two years ago.

"Absolutely. The results from the latest MRI scans show significant shrinkage in all four malignant areas of the brain and spine."

Grant breathed an audible sigh of relief while simultaneously praising Jesus. At his last hospital visit, the physicians had only given him a few weeks to live. Grant was definitely a fighter, though, and he was determined to not let his condition or the poor prognosis discourage him from a complete recovery. I had to admire his courage, and I was personally touched because I knew that his primary concern was not for his own life, but for mine. He did not want to leave me alone and afraid in the world, especially not *now* when I had finally found someone with whom to share my life. Someone who loved me in spite of my moodiness, my messiness, and my overall "lack of respect" for others, as I'd heard it put to me so many times before by the countless other men who had tried to take me in and help me "get on my feet." (Realistically, they were more interested in helping me get my feet in the air—men are such pigs!) But with Grant, it was different. Our relationship was in no way based on sex. I mean, sure, there had been a mutual physical attraction in the beginning, but that quickly cooled to a comfortable "bromance." He was a trusted friend whom I genuinely looked forward to coming home to each day after work. At the time, I was working as an intake clerk at the University of Pittsburgh's School of Dental Medicine.

During our time together, I woke up each day filled with energy, spirit, and life. A day seldom, if ever, passed without the stereo bumping and our bodies entangled in dances that easily rivaled the best moves in any Janet Jackson video. And he could always make me laugh. His willingness and ability to defy social norms or expectations made him an absolute delight to goof around with in public. One time, for example, he and I were waiting for the bus at an intersection when a fire truck pulled to a stop at the red light. Noticing the physical attractiveness of the firemen, Grant decided to yell out, "Hey, the fire's in my *pants!*" while gesturing obscenely at his crotch. The look on their faces was beyond priceless as their jaws literally dropped in astonishment. Grant and I laughed so hard that we nearly cried. But then, and much too quickly, things began to take a drastic turn for the worse.

It all started when Grant decided, upon his mother's wishes, to have a "routine" check-up regarding a benign tumor that had been removed from his cranium ten years ago, when he was just eleven years old. The doctor had advised yearly screenings to ensure proper healing of the brain tissue and to prevent any potential re-growth. Since all prior check-ups had yielded successful results, the doctor promised Grant that—should this screening come back clear—there would be no more need for future check ups. In other words, he would be considered cancer-free and fully cured!

Well, as our luck (fate?) would have it, there *was* a re-growth (or, as the doctor stated, "possibly a stem from the original tumor from ten years ago that I had missed"). In any event, the doctor advised *immediate* surgical removal of the stem, which had been biopsied as benign (not deadly). Personally, I found it highly suspicious that this doctor was also about to retire *forever* within the next two weeks, so of *course* he wanted to squeeze in that one last money-maker before hitting the golf courses of Tampa. Obviously, Grant was devastated by the news, and yet he steadfastly prepared himself for the operation. I remember feeling anxious about the impending procedure myself, as I began to worry that a major change may occur in his personality or attitude as a result of the surgery. As it turns out, my fears manifested to the fullest extent imaginable. I remember watching him bravely walk toward the hospital on the day of the operation. *What if this is the last time I see Grant?* I thought to myself. Well, it pretty much was the last time I saw the *real* Grant. The jovial, carefree, "fire's in my pants" Grant that I knew and loved transformed into a bitter, hostile, insecure, and venomous creature—almost overnight. When I would dance in the grocery store, for example, he would scold me, embarrassed to be seen with me. In my opinion, if an establishment does not condone dancing, they should not play dance music on the overhead speakers. For me, dance is almost involuntary—an automatic bodily response to musical stimuli. Besides, who was I hurting?

The night we came home from the hospital, he began having seizures reminiscent of Linda Blair's character in the most horrific scenes of *The Exorcist*. He would throw his head back and cackle in a demonic tone. He would then switch to desperate pleas for help, as though he knew that he was being somehow possessed by something unimaginably evil. At one point, he explained that God told him that his body would remain with me on earth, but that his soul was being taken up to heaven. He described the entrance process into the holy land as an audition in which he had to perform a song and dance of his choice for the Lord. He sang *Coming out of the Dark*, by Gloria Estefan, which was a popular track from her CD entitled *Into the Light*. An appropriate choice, for sure.

Apparently, the surgery that was conducted after ten years of remission had opened up Grant's brain and consequently made it vulnerable to "impurities," whether they were of the supernatural or microbiological type. In fact, the tiny benign stem aggressively mutated into a malignant *glioblastoma* tumor within two years, which spread down his spinal cord and neck with little or no hope of reversal, especially now that he weighed a measly 95 pounds (he was 5'11"). Chemotherapy would only destroy any healthy tissue that remained in his feeble body. But Grant wanted to try the chemo, anyway. He had completely lost his hearing in one ear, and one of his eyes had been surgically sewn shut due to an infection which was ominously spreading to his nose and throat. To be honest, I could not even look at him without wanting to break down and cry. But I knew I had to stay strong for his sake. I could not allow myself to crack.

So, as I'm sure you can imagine, I was overjoyed with the current news that the tumors were showing signs of improvement. It was just two weeks before Christmas. Was this our gift from God? That day at the hospital, he had his prescription filled for tramadol, (a "safer", non-narcotic alternative to percocets or other opiates).

There had been a very unpleasant incident in which Grant had tried to take his entire bottle of percocets, intranasally, and I was concerned that he may end up eventually hurting himself. "Mark my words, Grant. One of these days you are going to overdose on those pills and die." He dismissed my warnings with a cavalier attitude. The "new" Grant was one of no restraint or concept of moderation. In a word, he was a glutton. I remember coming home from work one afternoon to find him passed out on the couch, unconscious. In a panic, I repeatedly tried to wake him, to no avail. Finally I called 9-11, and just as the paramedics stepped into the room, Grant awoke in a rage.

"Daniel!" he should indignantly. "You're gonna get it! How dare you call these people and have me taken away! I wish it were *you* who had the brain tumor!" He then began shouting racist and homophobic slurs at the paramedics, referring to them as "niggers" and "faggots." Interesting, considering that Grant himself was both black *and* gay. The entire neighborhood gathered in the streets to witness the pathetic scene as the paramedics strapped him onto a stretcher and carried him toward the ambulance. It was humiliating. I asked a police officer, half-jokingly, if they could perform an exorcism on him at the hospital.

"I doubt it," he said, chuckling. "But I may be able to put you in contact with a priest."

Unfortunately, even after receiving the wonderful news about the tumor shrinkage, Grant decided to "celebrate" by crushing and snorting his entire bottle of pills in one evening.

"It's really not a good idea to be snorting *anything* considering you have this ongoing infection in your nose and throat," I warned him.

"Shut up and get away from me! It's my business and I'll do whatever I want!"

Deciding to respect his wishes (after all, I really did want him to enjoy the time he had left), I washed my hands of the situation and quietly went to lie down in the bedroom. A few hours later, I entered the living room, where I found him smoking a cigarette peacefully on the couch.

"I'm sorry for that outburst earlier," he smiled at me. I beckoned him to come to the bedroom, at which point he lay down next to me and went to sleep by the warm glow of the Christmas tree in the window. A few hours later, he started snoring, loudly. I tried to wake him up, but I could not rouse him. *Should I call 9-11?* I had flashbacks of the last time I did that. He had been so angry at me. I decided to let him sleep. A few minutes, later, the snoring abruptly ceased as he rolled on top of me, lifeless. In a total panic, I called 9-11 and they told me to try artificial respiration. I breathed into his mouth, and as I pushed in his abdomen he coughed up about a half gallon of blood all over me and the carpet. When the medics arrived, they tried to revive him, but it was too late. At the young age of twenty-four, Grant was gone.

As I looked helplessly upon his lifeless body that night, I was particularly captivated by the silver belt buckle that glistened around his waist. It simply and eerily read "TEMPERANCE: The ability to take in all things with a sense of moderation; self-control."

CHAPTER 1

God, Grant Us the Serenity

"Coincidences are God's way of remaining anonymous."
—*Albert Einstein*

Everything that happened to Grant, although certainly tragic, can be made directly analogous to what is happening on a macrocosmic/global scale right now. Because Grant was obviously unable to accept *himself* (remember the way he maliciously used the pejorative words "faggot" and "nigger"?), the cancer gained control over his body and he perished. This is not merely a personal theory that I have created. Rather, it has been scientifically *proven* that the actual shape of a water molecule will change, provided that someone meditates over the water in question. If the experimental water is looked upon with love and affirmation, the water molecule will change into a brilliant, multifaceted crystal. If, however, the same water is regarded with disdain or contempt, it will actually mutate into a *cancer cell*. What is the human body comprised of, mostly? You got it—we are made mostly out of water (roughly 70%). By refusing to love himself, Grant allowed the cancer to consume him. The earth, by no coincidence (there really *are* no coincidences, after all), is also composed of approximately 70% water. Unless we as a global family can figure out a way to look upon each other with total love and acceptance, we as a people are doomed to suffer the same fate that Grant experienced. Currently, the world is in a state of crisis. War, violence, poverty, and disease abound. We are, in essence, building a collective tumor and are headed toward a global aneurism. Is this part of the "doomsday" that some have predicted based on the Mayan calendar, which ends on December 21, 2012?

Within each of us lies the power to change the world, one person at a time, by changing *ourselves*. I believe that—unless we can learn as individuals to love *fearlessly, selflessly, and unconditionally*—we soon will be faced with a catastrophic population crash of apocalyptic magnitude. In their book, *Generations: The History of America's Future, 1584-2069*, authors Neil Howe and William Strauss have isolated a time period between 2013 and 2029 as a time when our country will face the "greatest upheaval in American history." Remember Noah and the ark? Noah was able to survive the flood simply because he was found to be righteous in the eyes of God. Similarly, each of us is called to righteousness, and that means being able to look first upon your *true self* with unconditional love and acceptance. The ego (which is actually a *false* sense of self) is fragile and subject to deterioration. It is built upon ephemeral materials (your possessions, looks, money, current job, etc.) that are subject to change. Anyone who is identified with his or her ego is at the mercy of their moods, which soar and plummet depending on their current circumstances or the approval or disapproval of others. A compliment, for example, causes the ego to skyrocket, while an insult causes undo distress. Pride and shame are simply different sides of the same coin. Conversely, someone who identifies with his or her *true self* has constant, abiding peace, regardless of their situation or other people's reactions. God never changes! We all come from and return to the same source, which is unconditional love. Everything else is an illusion and therefore a distraction from the truth.

Grant's problem was that he could not accept his own race or sexuality. He grew up in the middle-class, mostly white suburbs of Pittsburgh, Pennsylvania. I am sure that he endured years of teasing and torment from his peers (kids can be so cruel, right?). Unfortunately, the reality is that most "little kids" just grow up into bigger kids. That is, their physical bodies may mature, but they seldom grow up spiritually and intellectually because they don't put forth the effort to change: "When I was a child, I spoke like a child, I thought like a child, I reasoned like a child. When I became a man, I gave up childish ways." (1 Corinthians 13:11).

Although gay people have made tremendous political strides since the days of Stonewall (1969), we are still a far cry from being treated as equals by our heterosexual counterparts. Imagine if there were absolutely no social stigma associated with homosexuality.

Undoubtedly, there would be a dramatic increase in the number of openly gay people in the world. How can we ever hope to ascend to the next level of human consciousness if we cannot even see past such superficial issues as skin color and sexuality? Many minorities themselves are guilty of the same thing through over-compensation. They become overly "proud" of being gay, or black, or whatever their minority status happens to be. Over-identification with *part* of oneself eventually leads to loss of the *whole* self. We are so much more than just a skin color or sexual orientation. We need to realize that we are all, underneath it all, the *exact* same person—*one* incarnation that is life itself. In fact, recent genetic studies indicate that the ancestry of all living human beings can be traced back to the *same* woman who lived in Africa 200,000 years ago. She has been dubbed "Mitochondrial Eve," our collective mother.

I vividly recall an incident on the bus in Los Angeles, where I eventually moved after Grant died. I was on my way to work, as usual. But on this particular day, a homeless (possibly schizophrenic) "bag lady" was enraged because she wanted to sit down but there were no more available seats on the bus. Rather than politely asking another passenger to offer up his seat, this irate woman tried to physically force a young black woman from her seat on the bus. I will never forget the hateful things that spewed from her bitter tongue.

"Rosa Parks may have earned her place on the *bus*," the old hag screeched, "but she also earned her place in HELL! And Martin Luther King, Jr. is in hell, too! And you're going to the same place, you stupid bitch!" Well, after hearing these despicable words, I was appalled and simply could not remain silent.

"You are already *in* hell, my friend!" I shouted at her. Heaven and hell are not necessarily places that can be seen or visited, but rather a state of mind. By casting judgment on others, this woman was putting *herself* in a state of continual suffering. I once had a dream in which I was personally escorted through heaven and hell. Hell consisted of a giant, cascading waterfall made of *fire*, with millions of tiny, transparent bubbles descending from the fire-fall. Inside the bubbles were what appeared to be grotesque, mutilated faces with scrambled facial features. An eye was where the mouth should be, a mouth was where the ear should be, etc. These were the souls of the damned, who could do nothing but stay inside their own separate bubbles and look upon each other with disgust.

This dream taught me that "hell" is what happens when we cannot escape our own maddening thoughts, which keep us separated from one another. It is our constant attempt to make sense of the senseless. I recall another homeless man in L.A. who once told me to "Get out of your own head, Danny. It's a terrible place to be." Life itself is a paradox, and once you truly surrender to that fact, it frees your mind and allows you to be *present* and connected to the endless flow of joy that the universe provides. Animals are always present; they do not have a sense of the past or the future, which is why they are never depressed or dissatisfied with their lives. Interestingly enough, I was transformed into a dog when I traveled to "heaven" in my dreams. At that moment, I had no recollection of my life as Daniel, the human being. I was totally present, just barking and chasing my own tail. It was awesome!

Getting back to the woman on the bus, she turned to me and shouted, "I am NOT in hell! *You* are a faggot and you will be going to hell for sucking dick!" Bear in mind, this person knew absolutely nothing about me and was simply judging me based upon my physical appearance and/or my tone of voice. I am one of those guys that is not *always* assumed to be gay, necessarily, but if I choose to "come out" to someone, it is not usually a huge shock, either.

By this time, however, I was starting to become more than a little perturbed with this bitch. What right did this person have to spread her poison to a busload of unsuspecting, working-class citizens who were just trying to get to work on time? I think I must have blown a fuse at this point, because I responded with, "How many of you would support me in the decision to push this creature out the door and destroy it?" The bus was at full-throttle, traveling at approximately 50 mph down the freeway, and she was standing directly in the stairwell by the back door.

"Yeah! Do it! Do it!" everyone began chanting. Someone even had his video camera out, filming the entire drama. I am glad that I did not give into my own rage at that time. I was still level-headed enough to weigh out the potential consequences of my actions. I certainly did not want to spend the rest of my life behind bars over someone like her. Luckily, at the very next stop, she fled the scene, arms flailing in the air and cackling like the witch she was. Unreal.

When I got to work, I was further reprimanded, subtly, by a coworker because of the hand-woven, Jamaican hat I was wearing.

He looked at me for a moment, and then he asked another coworker, right in front of me, if she would ever dye her hair blonde. When she said "no!" he responded with, "Why not? Maybe because you are a dark-skinned Latina?" I knew this comment was directed at me, since I was a white boy who was wearing a "black man's" hat. A few minutes later, when I had a private moment with him in the kitchen, I simply said, "I think she'd look good with blonde hair."

Yet another time, while working at that same restaurant, I was waiting on two well-dressed, well-mannered women who kept complimenting me. "What a handsome young man. I can tell you believe in Jesus, you are so sweet," on and on. As it turned out, they were actually two neo-Nazis who were trying to recruit me to join the Klan. I couldn't believe it. Once I served them their dessert, they started bad-mouthing my other coworkers, most of whom were Hispanic. "See how they are taking away all of our jobs? It won't be long until they take over the world, as well! We have to stop them! But don't let them know how you truly feel about them, dear. You must keep your white cloak in your closet!" I was rendered speechless. I had to excuse myself from the table, at which point I actually broke down in tears. This was 2010, and people were still this narrow-minded? Seriously?

It was about this time in Los Angeles that I began to realize that there is an *Unholy* Spirit that looms in the world at this time. The Bible refers to it as the antichrist, the "reign of the beast." I do not believe that the antichrist is limited to one person. In fact, through my experiences in L.A., I personally witnessed more than a few demonic possessions. I saw people whose bodies were quite literally overtaken by this Unholy Spirit. The Bible specifically refers to this: "I have decided to deliver *such* a one to Satan for the destruction of his flesh, so that his spirit may be saved in the day of the Lord Jesus." (1 Corinthians 5:5). Who among us is susceptible to such possession and is it permanent? My personal answer is that just about anyone who is ego-driven and therefore not grounded in the *truth* can be at least temporarily, or possibly permanently, possessed by these demons. And they are very real. They are the antithesis of the *truth.* Christ represents the way, the truth, and the life. Anyone who does not live by the truth is not grounded and is subject to the destruction of his spirit—and that means being disconnected from eternal life. There are only two possibilities that exist: You are either *one* (that is, part of the one, universal spirit, a.k.a. the "collective conscience") or you are the *other* (disconnected from eternal life). Within each individual there is the potential to be a Christ figure or to be an antichrist. And it all starts with our willingness to be *honest* with ourselves in *all* aspects of ourselves. There is never a reason to be ashamed of what you are. Again, racism and homophobia are two of the greatest barriers that prevent this from happening.

It is common knowledge that "everybody lies." In fact, it is said that the average person lies nearly a dozen times a day. This has become acceptable, despite the fact that just about everyone also agrees that lying is morally wrong. This is pure insanity! There are really only two reasons that people lie: greed and fear. Lies are always told in an effort to somehow protect oneself from undesirable repercussions, but a single lie creates a domino effect of more lies, and before you know it your life has become nothing more than an on-going farce, a sham. Lies ultimately strip you of your happiness and your personal freedom because you are no longer free to be who you are. Instead, you are too concerned with what others may think of the real you. This completely empowers the *other*, while disempowering you and disconnecting you from your true, God-intended self. The other person, then, becomes an idol whom we strive to impress, a false-god. This directly violates the very first commandment that was given to Moses: "I am the Lord your God, you shall have no other gods before me" (Exodus, 20:3). This is just another way of saying "Just be your *true* self." In order to reconnect with your true self, you must first forget about your ego (the false self) and you must forget about the *other*.

Within each individual, there seems to be an on-going power struggle between wanting to "fit in" (be accepted by others) while at the same time wanting to "stand out" (be a unique individual). Both of these extremes, however, use other people's reactions as a way of gauging your own sense of self-worth. You are either conforming or rebelling to whatever cultural standards by which you were raised to live. That's why it says "blessed are the persecuted," in the Bible (Matthew 5:10). Those who are persecuted never really fit in anywhere. Eventually, they learn to find and love their true selves despite the constant rejection from other people. What was once a curse becomes an infinite blessing.

CHAPTER 2

I'm Your Venus

"I'm tough, ambitious, and I know exactly what I want. If that makes me a bitch, OK."

—Madonna

It is no secret that, in the population, crystal meth usage is disproportionately higher among gay men. What do you suppose the reason is for this phenomenon? While a lot of it may have to do with meth's aphrodisiacal qualities, I think that's only a small part of the equation. After all, straight people enjoy sex just as much as gay people do, so wouldn't *any* sexually active person want the party to last longer, feel better, and result in a more intense orgasm? More likely than not, meth is highly attractive to gay men because, as a group, they tend to suffer from abnormally low self-esteem. This is due to a number of factors, which collectively make up what I refer to as the "Gay Man's Inferiority Complex" (GMIC). Unfortunately, institutions such as religious fundamentalism and widespread heterosexism condition gay men to believe that they are somehow weaker or inferior to heterosexuals. Crystal meth, then, provides them with a temporary, false sense of confidence. This type of psychological damage is incurred at a very young age and is therefore difficult to undo or overcome.

For example, many gay youth choose not to come out to their families because they fear disownment or rejection on some level. While love itself is, by definition, *unconditional,* many parents do not demonstrate unconditional love toward their children. Rather, children are rewarded or punished according to their deeds, which often leads them to become dishonest with their parents: "I'll tell mom and dad whatever they want to hear, so I can get whatever I want and so they will adore me!" It is also extremely common for openly gay (or effeminate young men in general) to be ostracized by their peers, especially during high school or adolescence. Being called a "faggot" is the most degrading and humiliating thing a pubescent boy can be labeled as. This type of name-calling is often prevalent in high school environments simply because most of these adolescents are insecure about their *own* sexuality and therefore want to avoid being labeled as "gay" themselves. And it's always easier to point the finger at a physically smaller/weaker target like myself. Believe me, I have suffered more than my share of hazing and abuse as both a child and an adult, as you will see in the following chapters of this book. At 5'5" and 115 pounds, I make quite an easy target for homophobic "bullies" who cannot accept their own homosexual feelings. My physical appearance seems to appeal to all types of men, universally. (I couldn't possibly begin to count the number of supposedly "straight" men whom I've messed around with.) When a man who identifies as heterosexual sees me, it often conjures up repressed, unwanted feelings toward another man that he is not ready to deal with yet. This, in turn, causes feelings of rage and self-hate to emerge on a subconscious level and I, or someone like me, becomes the victim of this repressed rage through physical or verbal abuse. "Hate crimes" are very commonly directed toward gay men (remember Matthew Shepard, may he rest in peace?).

I recall a humorous story that one of my girlfriends once told me about her ex-husband. While they were still married, her husband had been spending a lot of time with his best friend, Nathan. One night, while her husband was asleep next to her in bed, he rolled over on top of her and put his arm around her. In a half-asleep, dreamlike state, he embraced her and then uttered the words, "Oh, Nathan .... It is in our dreams that the subconscious reveals itself. Our dreams are visualizations of our subconscious thoughts. Obviously, her husband was having an erotic dream about his best friend, Nathan.

There was a well-known psychologist by the name of Kinsey who devised a scale of human sexuality in 1948, and his research concluded that sexuality is on a gradient, a sliding scale. Interestingly enough, he also concluded that virtually *nobody* is exclusively heterosexual. Rather, we are all bisexual to varying degrees. So ladies, if you are dating a man who tells you that he has absolutely no gay fantasies or tendencies, you can pretty much guarantee that he is lying to you. If Kinsey's findings are in any way accurate, why do so many men continue to deny that part of themselves that is naturally attracted to other men? Clearly, it is because it makes them feel *inferior*. "Why would I need to look to another man for affection or emotional support of any kind, when God created me a man myself?" is the typical straight man's mindset. They fail to realize that being a "man" has nothing to do with who you are attracted to or who you are fucking. Being a "man" means being completely *honest* with yourself and others, and treating others with *respect*. (Remember the Golden Rule? It's such a simple concept, yet we all tend to forget about it sometimes.) At least openly gay men are man enough to admit that they like dick!

In truth, we all start out as *female* on the biological level. In fact, the word "girl" originally referred to *any* child. And we are all, of course, children of God, who is the only real man! Therefore, we are all, in essence, a little girl who is preparing to grow in grace and love in order to eventually reunite with her creator. We are all sleeping beauty, just waiting to awake inside.

In his book, *Finding the Boyfriend Within*, Brad Gooch argues that gay men need not search outside of themselves in order to find the perfect man. Rather, through careful introspection and self-reflection, you can find the perfect partner within yourself. Once you accomplish that, it opens you up to a whole new world of relationships with others as well. I would like to take Gooch's hypothesis a little further. True freedom from loneliness is possible only when we as gay, straight, or bisexual men are able to liberate the chained up little girl inside ourselves, the *goddess within*. In other words, we must learn to think with our heads and our *hearts*. The heart itself can actually function just like the brain. If someone has a heart transplant, he may develop the thoughts and personality traits similar to those of his donor's!

Men *can* learn to think with their hearts, but only through life experiences and the relationships we foster while we are here. The Bible is a great roadmap to the truth, but it is no substitute for real-life experience. Staying at home alone, reading your Bible all day will get you nowhere, spiritually. Through access to education and politics in this, the "information age," women have become empowered and liberated. They have been afforded, through struggles and triumphs (think: Betty Ford, Hillary Clinton, Oprah Winfrey), the same rights and privileges that men have enjoyed for centuries. The "system" can teach someone how to think—that is, how to use his/her brain. While the information age has been extremely beneficial to the women's rights movement, it has actually *prevented* men from achieving the same type of liberation because it tends to neglect or even replace matters of the heart.

In the beginning, God created us each "male and female" (Gen. 1:26-27). What this means is that we were once androgynous beings with equally masculine and feminine characteristics. As the universe tends to unfold, it spirals into a circular pattern with no beginning and no end. As it was in the beginning, so shall it be in the end. In other words, the universe is *cyclical*. This is why the Bible states that "the last shall be first and the first shall be last" (Matthew 20:16). We were *first* created as androgynous demigods with the power and freedom to roam and rule the universe. But through social conditioning and programming, we have forgotten our true, original selves and lost our divine powers. I spoke earlier of an impending population crash. Who will survive? My guess is that it will be those who can fuse their masculine and feminine energies together; those who can use both the left and right sides of their brains equally. We will then be able to return to the androgynous beings that we were originally made to be. Women, who go through a monthly *cycle*, are naturally more in touch with their bodies and the rhythm of life. All human life on earth, after all, comes from the female. For this reason, women have an innate ability to think with their hearts. Their maternal instincts often compel them to be naturally intuitive and nurturing.

I often refer to myself as the goddess, Venus, in the form of a man (Venus with a penis, if you will). In many cultures, men have been brainwashed to be ashamed of their feminine sides, to deny the inner goddess. Some of this "macho" thinking has changed slightly in recent years through the metrosexual movement. The TV show, *Queer Eye for the Straight Guy*, for example, showcases heterosexual men who embrace their softer sides through high-fashion, poise, and traditionally "feminine" tastes in décor. All of these efforts are made, however, with the express purpose of trying to attract a woman. In other words, the metrosexual man follows the gay man's advice for one reason: to get laid. This is a very masculine (and selfish!) angle and does little, if anything, to help the man get back in touch with his inner goddess. Even gay men may not be as in touch with their feminine sides as they'd like to believe they are. They often impersonate the "diva," that is, the domineering, controlling woman. This is simply the liberated woman who is expressing her *masculine* side. Madonna, the quintessential liberated woman, once stated, "I'm tough, ambitious, and I know exactly what I want. If that makes me a bitch, OK."

Embracing your feminine side means allowing yourself to be nurturing and giving. Many gay guys won't even date another guy if they are both "tops." This shows you just how selfish men can be when it comes to relationships. Any relationship—gay or straight—that is based on sex will eventually fail. Gay marriage will not prove to be a viable solution because modern couples (gay or straight) do not really respect the sanctity of marriage and do not keep the vows they take at the altar. (So what's the point in taking the vows at all?) A divorce is a relatively easy way out. With the exception of unforeseen abuse, there is no problem that cannot be worked through. Filing for "irreconcilable differences" is the quickest way for most couples to resolve an on-going sense of dissatisfaction. The whole point of taking those vows is to say, "This love is worth more to me than my own sense of immediate pleasure or happiness." It's about self-sacrifice, to "lay down your own life for a friend," as Jesus said (John 15:13). It means standing by your partner through good times *and* bad, in sickness and in health (ring any bells?).

Access to information allows the woman to regain her masculine self. It empowers her with the tools to take control of her life and her relationships, to be the "man" whenever necessary by making logical, pragmatic decisions. Conversely, the information age has also led to a breakdown in interpersonal communication and genuine relationships (matters of the heart). Texting, for example, has become a cheap substitute for a telephone conversation in which two people have a chance to engage in an unfettered, heart-to-heart talk. One-sentence emails have replaced handwritten letters, written and signed with love. Isolation and loneliness abound as we spend more time with machines (our PCs) than we do with each other. This has ultimately led to the decline and dissolution of what "might have been" in terms of new and creative relationships. This is what Jesus means when he says "Whenever two or more of you are *gathered* in my name, there am I in your midst" (Matthew 18:20). The physical *togetherness* of people allows for a third, unique entity to be co-created that did not exist before. That entity is called a *relationship* and it exists eternally (just as "God" is an eternal, infinite entity).

Crystal meth and other substances are often used to combat the loneliness and isolation that result from the impersonal information age in which we live. After Grant's tragic demise, I was left feeling desperately alone and depressed. I had built the last three years of my life around being his caretaker, his support system during his crisis. Once he was gone, I was left feeling unsure of my own role in life. I started to feel suicidal. Although I had been totally sober for over three years, I found myself again searching for the drug that would lift my spirits. And I began putting myself in extremely dangerous situations in order to get it. My usual method to score the drug was by going on-line and meeting gay men who would "smoke me out" in exchange for sexual favors. One of these men, in particular, proved to be highly toxic to me. I had never injected meth before in my life, but he pressured me into it and administered a nearly lethal dose. I could do nothing but lay there, motionless, for hours and pray as my heart raced. When I refused to see him after that, he angrily announced that he had "killed my boyfriend." This was evidence to me that the same demon was again following me. The demon that had destroyed Grant was determined to destroy me as well, if I allowed it to do so.

My first impulse was to flee the situation and remove myself from this evil man. I decided to move to Los Angeles, where I had lived five years ago as a gay porn star and escort. I knew that meth would be highly accessible there, and it soon became my mission to embark on a journey of reckless substance abuse abandon. It was during this excursion that I learned how to free the goddess within. Sometimes, the only way to find the light is by stumbling around, searching for it desperately in the darkness. Through my relationships with people and through divine intervention, I learned just what it meant to love fearlessly, selflessly, and unconditionally.

It says in the Bible to "Be not forgetful to entertain *strangers*: for by this some have entertained *angels unawares*" (Hebrews 13:2). This clearly means that angels can assume human form and dwell among us. By really paying attention while I was in L.A., I became *aware* of the angels who surrounded me and the messages they were sent to give me.

The Mayan calendar has isolated the time period between June 8th, 2004 and June 6, 2012 as a "time of preparation" in which light (good) and darkness (evil) will engage one another in unchecked struggles of equal ferocity. (Both of these dates mark a Venus eclipse, in which the planet Venus moves between the sun and planet Earth.) Little did I know, I was about to encounter both forces, head-on. Through my own personal trials and tribulations in L.A, I was finally able to stop using meth because I began to realize that I was, in fact, much stronger I thought I was. My weakness guided me toward my ultimate strength. I could finally say, with confidence, that I was one tough bitch!

A long-time friend and colleague of mine, Tim, invited me to stay with him in L.A. for two weeks in February, 2010. During that time with him in Santa Monica, CA, romantic feelings that I once had for him in college began to resurface. What stands out in my mind the most was the time he and I experimented with "mind synergy." We succeeded in making the song *Faithfully*, by Journey, come onto the radio simply by concentrating on that particular song and wishing for it to be played next. "Look what we can do together!" I shouted in disbelief when it actually happened. I thought that moving to L.A. may be a way to finally actualize a real relationship with him. At the time, I didn't realize that I was trying to use him as an emotional crutch. I had not yet begun my own process of healing. As most of us know, you cannot love someone else until you love yourself first. Tim invited me to move in with him for a while, to get a "fresh start" in life and a change of scenery. I accepted.

It was during my stay with Tim in L.A. that I began to notice and feel the direct presence and power of God like I had never known previously. I felt like I was exactly where I was supposed to be, that the universe was calling to me personally and thunderously—that I was part of something much bigger than myself. It became a roller coaster ride unlike anything I have experienced before or since, and it all happened within one year's time.

Are you ready?

Brace yourself, because when a lot of shit happens in a relatively short period of time, it's known as *fast-living*.

Looking back, I think I just may have lived at the speed of light.

Chapter 3

A Rough Beginning

After staying with Tim for those two weeks in February, I visited my parents in Georgia for three months before I was ready to return to L.A. It all began on that fateful day, May 10, 2010. I was embarking on this journey with little more than 500 dollars in my pocket—a measly settlement from an auto insurance company. My pickup truck had been rear-ended because I ran out of gas along a river-road in Georgia. Miraculously, there was a metal guardrail about 15 feet long in the exact place that I had broken down. If it hadn't been for that guardrail, my truck would have crashed into the river below. After the accident, my truck was unrecognizable, but I emerged unscathed. I remember feeling hopeful and excited about venturing out west again. There has always been something alluring about the West Coast. I'm not sure whether it's the sunshine, the beaches, or all that (legal!) marijuana. In any event, I was ready for a change and eager to start anew. With Tim on my side, what could possibly go wrong?

Those optimistic feelings were slightly challenged by the young man sitting next to me on the airplane. He handed me a small, leather-bound version of the New Testament and warned me that things were "about to get difficult" in my life. *About* to get difficult? I had just lost my boyfriend, my truck was now totaled, and I had been abruptly and ruthlessly discharged from my last job by my psychotic, bipolar boss. He was gay and clearly pissed off when he finally realized that I had no interest in even talking to him, much less sleeping with him. But there were also some words of encouragement from this man on the plane, who—looking back—I consider to be the first of many angels that I would encounter in Los Angeles, the "City of Angels."

"Take comfort in the Lord," he told me. "You will be faced with many hardships, but He will not forsake you. He has brought you this far for a reason and has a special design for your life."

Although I believed (or at least *wanted* to believe) that my dreamy blond college crush was finally ready to admit that he was in love with me, I quickly began to see that I had been misreading his signals. (Of course, it didn't help that we had messed around during my last visit). During those two weeks in February, he completely spoiled me. I felt like a princess, as though my every wish were his command. Once I actually moved in, however, I noticed an immediate shift in his demeanor. I started to feel like an unwelcome guest, a third wheel whenever his other friends would come over. I felt like I was somehow getting in the way, or that my overall energy was annoying to him. Clearly, he had no intentions of keeping me as a live-in lover. More than likely, he just wanted a local "fuck buddy" that he could drop in on whenever the mood struck. Feeling slighted and tired of being used for my body, I again turned to meth for a means of escaping the heartache and rejection I was feeling.

Although I had decided long ago that my days as a porn star were over, I accepted a role as a "top" in a bareback (condom-free) film. It was being shot by a director whom I'd worked for once, years ago. I bumped into him in the grocery store and he recognized me. So, armed with a bag of meth as ammunition, Danny Chance finally made his long-awaited comeback appearance in the oh-so classy flick, *Latino Cum-dumpster*. I remember the director saying to me that "sex is an addiction." He was correct. Most men are sex addicts, plain and simple. The more sex they get, the more they want. While I had been occupied with Grant for all those years, sex had taken a backseat to working, survival, and caretaking. I had actually, at one point, taken a *two year* hiatus from sex of any kind with anyone. I was beginning to think that maybe I was done with it permanently, that I had somehow outgrown it or cleansed it from my system. Well, as it turns out, I was wrong! After shooting the scene for that video, I went on a four-day sexcapade that involved more men than I care to remember. I was insatiable—possibly making up for lost time? During this four-day binge, I recall walking a ten mile stretch on Santa Monica Blvd. in the blistering sun, stopping only to refuel with water, Gatorade, or "liquid love." By the time I reached my destination, I had countless blisters on my feet, not to mention a very sore jaw!

I remember complaining to a coworker the next day about my sore *feet*. (I had just been hired as a waiter in an Italian restaurant.) This particular coworker stands out in my mind for a couple of reasons. She was a great trainer and a lovely person, physically. She seemed to suffer from an insidious ego problem, though, because she was over-identified with her performance at work. (Remember—it's not about what you *do*, it's about who you *are* that matters.) A guest with a cheese allergy asked her if the meatballs contained any cheese. She told them, "No, there's no cheese in the meatballs." Well, I simply pointed out to her, privately, that I had just finished reviewing the menu and that the meatballs were made with parmesan cheese. Her countenance immediately crinkled up as she stuttered, "I know that! I don't count the parmesan cheese. It's not real." Not *real?* I'm sure that the only thing that wasn't being real was *her.* From that day forward, she treated me like shit when I had only been trying to help her!

After I had saved a considerable amount of money in tips, Tim began pressuring me to move out and get my own place. As it would happen, another coworker of mine mentioned that she would be moving out of her apartment so that she could cohabitate with her new boyfriend (who also worked with us). She said I could sublet the unit from her, which was only four blocks away from the restaurant where we worked. It seemed like the perfect plan. After I successfully moved all of my belongings into the unit and had the utilities turned on, the landlord informed me that subletting the apartment was a direct violation of the lease, and that I would have to leave the premises within a week or else he was going to call the sheriff. Conveniently, the coworker who rented me the unit and her boyfriend had since quit their jobs at the restaurant and were nowhere to be found. I did not expect to be fucked over by a trusted coworker, and at this point I had nowhere to go. Clearly, Tim did not want me to move back in with him; he was overjoyed that I had finally left him to his privacy! I even offered to finish out the entire lease's obligation for her. She had been signed onto the unit for three more months, all of which I offered to pay for, upfront and in-full. I figured this would allow me adequate time to find other arrangements, since the landlord also informed me that my credit standards were not good enough to qualify as a tenant there, anyway. The landlord refused my offer. This just didn't make sense to me! I was offering to fully pay the amount owed on the lease, thereby fulfilling her financial obligations, and they were refusing to allow it. Was this some kind of personal conspiracy against me? Perhaps another homophobic slap in the face? "We don't want any faggots living in this building!"? Of course, there was no way to really *prove* any type of discrimination against me. So I did the only thing I could do: I gathered up my things and moved into a sober living facility in West Hollywood (the gay ghetto of L.A.).

This arrangement, again, proved to be nothing more than a scam devised to target gay people and steal their money so that the other residents could live there, rent free. I was concerned that the facility was not really suited to my needs in the first place because all of the other residents appeared to be straight men, all of them alcoholics. I was the only meth addict, and there was nobody there who could really relate to my situation. I was assured, however, that it was the perfect place for me. Would you believe that I stayed there for *one night* before they threw me out? The monthly rent there was $800, which I paid in-full prior to moving in. When I returned from work the next day, the property manager confronted me with the following question: "Did you have anything to drink last night? The other residents said that you clearly smelled of alcohol. You signed a document stating that you would abstain from all drugs and alcohol while living on these premises."

In all honesty, I *had* partaken in *one* beer the night before, but if my breath allegedly smelled of alcohol, why wouldn't they notify the property manager at that time, instead of waiting until the next day? In fact, I had spoken to him myself that night and he had suspected nothing. I'm convinced that the real reason the other residents chose to have me evicted was because they were hating on my sexuality. When I first moved in, no one seemed to assume that I was gay, although I'm sure some of them suspected it. When I was introduced to a female resident on my first night, she smiled and said, "My name's Michelle. It's easy to remember because I'm the only girl here."

"Really?" I laughed. "I thought *I* was the only girl here." My roommate also asked me if I was gay or straight, and I told him I was gay. So, by that point, any doubts that anyone may have had about my sexuality were completely removed. The very next day, I was literally pushed out the door onto the lawn, with all my belongings—at midnight. And no, they did not refund my $800. I thought the whole point of the facility was to *help* people? I had nowhere to go and practically no money left. I considered suing them, since they had absolutely no proof that I had been drinking the night before. I decided against it, though, because I knew they would ask me in court if I had been drinking. And you know how I feel about lying, especially under oath. Frustrated, pissed-off, and *again* feeling victimized, I scrolled through my cell phone until I located the phone number of someone who might be willing to help me. He was a middle-aged Asian man of Chinese decent, whom I will from here-on refer to as the "Chinese Tweaker." I had partied with him about a week or so before moving into the sober living home. He seemed to think such an establishment was probably not the best option for me. He assured me that, should the arrangement fall through, he would allow me to stay with him until I was able to make other arrangements. And, although I was impressed that he actually kept his word by allowing me to move in, I soon discovered that his goodwill gesture had little to do with concern for my personal welfare. He, like every other man, just wanted a piece of ass. I wasn't attracted to him at all, and it didn't take long for him to realize it, either. At that point, he began intentionally giving me the cold shoulder. He completely flipped his script! It was like I was living with a totally different person than the sweet, hospitable man I'd met on-line a few weeks ago.

"I don't want to make you feel too comfortable here," I remember him saying in an icy tone of voice. "And I will not accept any rent money from you, either, because that would legally entitle you to live here." In short, he wanted me out, ASAP. A real stand-up guy, right? Sure, he kept his word by allowing me to move in with him, but that's only because he didn't want to consider himself to be a liar. He obviously had no problem being an asshole, though! People are crazy. I tried to stay out of his way as much as possible. In fact, during the two short weeks that I stayed with him, I only spent *four* nights there. During the other ten nights, I was roaming the streets of Santa Monica Blvd. like a stray dog, high on meth and open to whatever other temptations happened to present themselves.

While staying with the Chinese Tweaker, I discovered a website that was constructed specifically for gay men who wished to meet other men for uninhibited, bareback sex. With each picture and profile, it specifically stated whether or not they "partied" (that is, whether or not they intended the sexual encounter to include crystal meth). As a means of avoiding the Chinese Tweaker, I spent innumerable hours on that website, meeting and getting high with sometimes five different guys in a single day. It was like an endless cesspool of online tweakers, many of whom I later realized were (quite literally) representatives of a race of satanic lords—an alien race of fallen angels who were now coming back to rule the world. They will rule the earth in what will soon become a hedonistic dystopia, rampant with overindulgences of every kind.

Remember the ancient Egyptian pharaohs? They were esteemed not merely just as kings, but as actual deities who planned to return to the earth during the end times. They were the gods of the underworld in human form. The practice of mummification was introduced as a means of preserving the pharaohs' bodies, so their souls could one day return to the earth and re-enter the same bodies they once inhabited. This plan proved to be faulty, of course, because—despite their best efforts—the bodies still decayed over time. The ancient gods of the underworld may not be able to return to their original bodies, but their souls *are* able to seize control of those human forms that *currently* inhabit the earth today. Who is susceptible to being overtaken by, say, Osiris? My answer: Those who serve little or no purpose in society, yet remain ungrounded and weak-minded. Selfish men who spend their days searching for pleasures of the flesh and ego (drugs, sex, material gain). Men who do not have families or loved ones who depend on them or would notice any type of change in their behavior or appearance. Generally, it is only the eyes (the "windows to the soul") that appear remarkably different after the demonic transformation has occurred. Eyes that were once soft and dilated become replaced by beady, shifting "cameras" that send images and information back to Lucifer, king of these satanic beasts. The memories of the original person are downloaded by the demons to ensure an easy transition once they infiltrate the bodies.

Over time, I learned that I had somehow gained the devil's favor, because—despite the potentially lethal situations I found myself in—I always managed to escaped, unharmed. It was as though even the devil himself were powerless over me. I had charmed the snake, so my own soul remained safely intact in its original body. Just like the Old Testament prophet, Daniel, who was thrown into the lion's den, the Lord God sent his angels to protect me by "sealing the lion's jaws;" I was found to be innocent in the eyes of God.

There are also those people who *unknowingly* serve Satan by acting as "worker bees." They have helped to build an empire that is both comfortable and conducive to the hedonistic lifestyles enjoyed by the satanic lords. The worker bees have been programmed, through thought-insertion, to believe that they have goals or dreams of their *own*, but in reality, they are only acting as puppets to the master of deceit. He is using them to do his handy work: to build machines, buildings, gadgets and weapons that will allow his race of fallen angels to "live it up" in a world they themselves conceptualized but did not put in the physical labor to construct. Once they are done using these worker bees, they leave them to die, probably so they can feed on their rotting flesh beneath the soil.

I vividly recall meeting the first of these fallen angels from the aforementioned bareback website. Although this "person" had no job, no income, and no daily routine or apparent purpose in life, he appeared to live in splendid and decadent conditions. His apartment was replete with priceless statues and exquisite antiques; breathtaking artwork adorned the walls and ceilings. The thing that I remember most of all was the giant, hanging sign that was prominently displayed above his bed, which proudly read "SINNER." The bedroom itself was reminiscent of an old-time gothic cathedral, bedecked in red velvet linens and golden candelabrums. Classical music played softly in the background. At the time, of course, I thought he was just a regular guy with eclectic taste. After offering me the proverbial "peace pipe," we engaged in hours of ungodly acts of fornication, all of which I thoroughly enjoyed.

I left his place feeling slightly guilty and depraved regarding my actions. Could one drug cause me to perform such acts of indiscretion, or was there something within my own being that needed to release these feelings? Perhaps the drug just gave me the excuse (and the energy) to go through with it? As I was pondering these questions, I happened to walk past the street where my ex-boyfriend of five years ago lived. I had not spoken to Darrell since our (very unpleasant) falling out. In fact, I still have the scars on my right hand from the day I shattered his bedroom window with my fist. (I was actually aiming for his face, but he moved away and I guess I'm a lousy shot!) The reason I was so upset was because he had insisted that I move in with him, but soon replaced me with another boy once he was tired of fucking me. We met at a local dance club in West Hollywood that featured retro-pop music, my personal favorite. I just never get tired of old-school Madonna or Michael Jackson. The more I hear it, the more I like it. I swear, music really *is* the only healthy addiction! Well, after two weeks of incredible sex and equally incredible cocaine, neither one of us wanted the party to end.

It was through my relationship with Darrell that I first started to learn what love was *not*. A lot of people (men in particular) mistake lustful obsession for love. Sure, Darrell and I had some great sex, but that's about *all* we had in common. He continually made me feel as though I was somehow less than he was because I didn't have an expensive car, or a respectable job, or a chic group of friends as my entourage. In fact, he would always make up an excuse as to why I couldn't join him for an evening out on the town with his friends. Was I an embarrassment to him because I was a porn star that someone might recognize? Did he not want to be associated with such trashiness? As I always say, anybody who *watches* porn (or engages in casual sex of any kind for that matter) is no different than the person in the video. After all, God sees everything, whether it's on camera or not. That's why Jesus says, in regards to the whore who is about to be stoned to death, "Let he without sin cast the first stone" (John 8:7). All of us are born with the same chains of sin wrapped around us. Only the strong can break free of these shackles and transcend our current status as mere *creations* to actualize our innate ability to be *creators*; to "be perfect, even as God is perfect," as Jesus states (Matthew 5:48). In the book of Genesis, it says that we were made in God's image, meaning that we are a direct reflection of divine power and light with the unlimited potential to succeed.

I did wind up visiting Darrell that day, mainly to apologize for my irrational behavior and to make sure that he harbored no resentment toward me. As usual, he was intoxicated when I arrived; he was still a raging alcoholic, apparently. He assured me that all was forgiven, and that he still loved me. I suspected, however, that it was merely the alcohol talking and he was horny and hoping for some sex. I may have allowed that to happen, had I not just finished relieving myself at the "SINNER's" place. My suspicions were soon confirmed when he stopped returning my calls/texts a few days later. *Probably for the best,* I thought smugly. At least my conscience was clear.

Chapter 4

The Building Calls Me Back

I was starting to feel slightly homesick for my beloved Shih Tzu, Peppy, who was still in Georgia with my parents. So I decided to apply as a tenant in the same building that I had moved into years ago after Darrell had thrown me out of his place. I knew that I had left the building on decent terms, and that they welcomed pets there. Despite my heinous credit record, I was somehow approved and was permitted to move into the building on 7th street in Koreatown. I did not have my own transportation this time, though, and I knew that getting to work on the bus would take a good hour, one direction. But given the current circumstances, it seemed to be my only option. I wanted to remove myself from the Chinese Tweaker ASAP. A week after my application was approved, I moved into apartment 410. It was a charming studio complete with hardwood floors, exposed brick walls, and giant bay windows treated with wooden blinds. It had a fully-equipped kitchen and bathroom. Finally, my own sanctuary, after three months of floundering around in limbo. By the time I furnished the landlord with the rent check, I was literally penniless. Prior to moving in with the Chinese Tweaker, two of my front teeth had broken off and it cost me nearly $3,000 to fix have them fixed. It is common knowledge that meth will destroy your teeth. Even that, unfortunately, was not enough to deter me from using.

The first day I moved into my apartment, in fact, I visited a nearby bathhouse. For those of you who don't know what a bathhouse is, it's essentially a private men's club where guys go to have anonymous sex with each other. Everyone walks around in nothing but a towel. Crystal meth is ubiquitous in such places, which is why I was there, of course. I wanted to score some free drugs. There were very few other patrons there that day, but I ended up meeting a man in his mid-to-late forties named Paul, who promised me that he could hook me up provided that I was willing to pitch in some cash. We left the bathhouse together after he contacted his dealer. During our conversation, I remember connecting with him because we both expressed our disgust with people's dishonesty. Who can you trust these days? Everyone we had met had an angle, it seemed. Nobody was interested in a genuine friendship or even knew *how* to be a friend, we agreed. People just used each other for their own selfish agenda and then cast them aside like a worn out pair of sneakers. Paul did make good on his word to acquire the crystal meth (which was quite potent stuff if I recall correctly!), and we seemed to hit it off rather well during our initial high. As any seasoned tweaker can tell you, though, the high does not last forever. When people start to "come down," they usually get irritable and paranoid. While he was in the shower, I took it upon myself to look through his wallet. After all, this was a stranger in my house; I felt I had a right to know his information just in case he decided to steal from me or something. I wasn't entirely sure that he wasn't homeless or some sort of con-artist, either. As I looked at his I.D., I realized that it was not *him* in the picture at all, nor was the person's name "Paul" who was pictured. It was "Alonzo Ruiz," or something—clearly a Hispanic name. "Paul" was a grey-haired white man. All of the credit cards in his wallet bore the exact same name, "Alonzo Ruiz." Did Paul steal this man's wallet? Or worse, did he mug or murder someone in order to steal his identity? Paranoid and completely tweaked out, I decided to confront Paul when he finished his shower.

"May I ask you a question?" I said.

"Sure, ask me anything."

"Is it OK if I see your I.D.?" I half-expected him to say that he didn't have one, but I knew that in order to gain entrance into the bathhouse each member was required to present a valid form of I.D.

"Of course," he smiled, nonchalantly. When he handed me the card, I glanced at it for a moment and then looked back up at Paul.

"This isn't you," I said flatly.

"Yes, it is," he replied, a confused look on his brow.

"No, it's not."

"Yes, it is," he repeated, this time a little more annoyed. He paused for a moment, and then, as though a light bulb went off in his head suddenly, he laughed nervously and exclaimed, "Oh! I know why you are saying that! "Paul" isn't my *real* name, it's my nickname. That really is me in the picture, though."

Now, first of all, what kind of a nickname is "Paul" when someone's given name is "Alonzo?" In fact, what kind of nickname is "Paul," at all? Obviously he was sill trying to bullshit me, so I decided to go for the jugular.

"Listen," I said. "I will give you one last chance to tell me the truth (wasn't this the same guy who hated liars?) and then I'm going to have to ask you to leave."

"It's really my I.D.," he insisted. "I give you my word."

"Really?" I asked, clearly pissed. "If that's the case, then why does it say 'brown' under 'eye color' on this license, and yet I'm staring at someone who has light blue eyes?"

At this point, he knew there was no more denying it. He was full of shit. I had completely cornered him in a lie that he could no longer cover up. So he did the only thing he could: he became extremely hostile toward me.

"You know I ought to beat the shit out of you, you stupid little bitch! I thought you were my friend!" As he uttered these cruel and hateful words, I saw him transform into a rotting corpse, right in front of my eyes. I will never forget it, as it haunts me still. Lies lead to death and destruction, and what I witnessed was his impending death, which flashed before my eyes in one clairvoyant moment. "I'm outta here!" he screamed, as he violently stormed out the door and down the staircase (much to my relief, of course). I was glad to be rid of him. God only knew what he was capable of! Once he was locked securely outside of the building, I waited in the lobby to make sure he was really gone for good. I didn't want him re-entering the building to harass me if another tenant happened to enter or exit the building, leaving the door ajar.

A few moments later, a very handsome young man entered through the door and smiled a very "come-hither" smile at me. Still traumatized from my exchange with Paul, I simply shook my head. "No?" inquired the stranger, who was removing a motorcycle helmet from his head, revealing his beautiful dark hair underneath.

I briefly explained to him that there was a con-artist stalking me outside the building and I asked him to check and see if the man was still lurking about the premises.

"Let me handle this," he said, in his best knight-in-shining-armor voice. He then exited the building. Still inside the foyer, I could hear him talking to Paul and ordering him to leave the property immediately, before he had to notify the authorities. *What a nice guy!* I thought to myself.

"My name's Ron," said the sexy stranger as he re-entered the building. "I live in apartment 409."

"Oh, really? I'm Daniel, and I just moved into apartment 410, directly across the hall from you. I used to live in this building years ago, on the 2nd floor."

"Ah, so the building called you back, then?" he smiled.

"I guess you could say that."

"Well, if you ever need anything else, I'm right across the hall. Drop in anytime you like. Peace and love, man."

"Thank you so much," I gushed. "It was great meeting you." *Wow, what an amazing guy*, I thought to myself. *I definitely wouldn't mind getting to know him a little bit better . . . .* Well, as it turns out, I would get to know him a *lot* better, but we'll get to that part of the story soon enough.

About a week or so after that episode with Paul, I decided to once again get online and see what sort of trouble I could get myself into. After briefly chatting with a guy who lived in West Hollywood ("Weho," as the locals commonly call it), he invited me over for a fun-filled day of porn, sex, and drugs—all at his expense. How could I say no? Upon arriving at his apartment complex, I began to have second thoughts, though. He told me to text him when I got there, which I did. But, rather than have me ring the doorbell like a normal person would, he suggested that I simply let myself into his apartment, where I would supposedly find him in the bedroom. I was not comfortable with such a plan because I had not yet seen him in person and I had no idea what I might encounter. When I asked him to come to the door, he hesitated briefly, and then insisted that I meet him in the alley behind the building instead. Now, this rose more than a few red flags. Was he planning to have me jumped or mugged? Why on earth could he not just answer the door? Did he not even live at this address?

Clearly, this was some sort of a set-up that I was unwilling to pursue any further.

I politely thanked him over the phone for inviting me and then quickly fled the scene. Well, as it would happen, on my way back home I bumped into an acquaintance of mine named Joe whom I'd met a few weeks earlier at a twenty-four-hour café in Weho. I had just finished a night of dancing and decided to stop there for a bite to eat. Joe was from the Midwest and had moved to L.A. in hopes of becoming a successful actor or movie star. But so far, Lady Luck was not on his side. He was squatting in a dilapidated, condemned house that had no amenities or utilities. He survived by stealing food from grocery stores and turning tricks, mainly. I was appalled and saddened by the conditions in which he lived. He seemed like a nice enough kid, so I did what I considered to be the right thing: I invited him to stay with me. We spent several hours together before finally bussing back to Koreatown. The whole time, we got along famously—laughing, joking, in general having a great time together.

All that changed when we entered my apartment and smoked a little bit of weed and meth together. His first words (though it didn't sound like his voice at all anymore) were, "I'm in, now." He then began spouting off maniacal rants of epic proportions, his eyes turning red and practically bulging out of his head. He physically began to close in on me, all the while shouting biblical warnings of Sodom and Gomorrah, fire and brimstone. I was terrified. What I remember most was when he cried out, "The rock will be taken from you, and those who depend upon it shall be cast into the lake of fire!" (By "rock," I'm sure he was referring to meth.) He also confessed that he had sexually molested several underage boys. Clearly, there was a demon within him (or was it within the building itself?). At first, I was convinced that the building was haunted. It is over 100 years old, after all. If those walls could talk, I wonder what they would say. (Probably something like, "Wash me, please! I'm covered in crack smoke and semen stains!") As Joe narrowed in on my trembling body, his demonic tone increased in volume and intensity—a crescendo of sheer poetic insanity. Then, just as suddenly as it had begun, he fell silent and returned to the "old" Joe I had eaten with a few hours ago at the local IHOP.

"I'm gonna do my laundry," he said casually. "The machines are in the basement, right?" I nodded, confused. He then left the apartment to do his laundry downstairs, at which point I followed him.

"Do you mind telling me what in the hell all that was about?" I asked, still shaking.

"What all *what* was about?" he replied ignorantly. He had no recollection of anything he had said or done.

"Is it true that you have sexually molested underage boys?" He looked surprised, and then sighed, ashamed.

"That wasn't me who did that. It was the devil *inside* me." Without further adieu, I asked him to leave the building. I was not prepared to deal with someone like him. Thankfully, he finished his laundry and reluctantly returned to Weho. I never saw him again after that.

Chapter 5

Naked Neighbors

After my unsettling encounters with Paul and homeless Joe, I suffered from a severe ear and throat infection, probably a consequence of having been awake for at least five consecutive days. I decided right then that I should probably take a break from smoking meth for a while. After I recovered from the illness, I continued to go about my day-to-day business, which included going to work and decorating my new pad with furniture and artwork. Everything seemed to be in order, at last. That is, until I met Nicole. She was a 21-year-old model who also lived in the building (or at least, her brother did), and she had an insane addiction to marijuana. I had met more than a few crack whores in my day, but a weed-whore? I guess anything is possible . . .

One day as I was smoking a cigarette on the fire escape, she approached me and asked if I smoked weed, which of course, I do. When I offered to smoke her out, her gorgeous brown eyes lighted up with glee. As we blazed together in my apartment, she took it upon herself to be the designated D.J. After all, what's good weed without good music? It just so happens that she selected a Stevie Wonder song, *Superstitious,* (one of my personal favorites). As we danced and sang together, I shared the following story with her:

I had won a pair of tickets to see Mr. Wonder in concert at the Melon Arena in Pittsburgh one time. I was the seventh caller to phone the radio station when they played one of his songs (*Signed, Sealed, Delivered*). When the radio D.J. asked me who I'd be taking with me to the show, I told him that it would be my best friend, Grant, who was battling brain cancer. "If Stevie can't lift our spirits, who can?" I remember saying.

When Stevie first set foot on stage, he explained the reason for the tour. He was not on the road to promote an album (there was no album to promote!). Rather, he explained that his beloved mother, who had just recently passed away, appeared to him in a dream and gave him the following instructions: "Stevie," she said, "I want you to get your butt out there on the road to let people know that death cannot separate those people who truly love one another." Grant, who could barely stand up or walk at that point, cheered boisterously from his seat. The concert itself was an affirmation of love; it was as if I could feel the Holy Spirit surrounding the stadium walls with a warm embrace. Two weeks later, Grant was dead.

As Nicole and I got better acquainted with one another, she confessed to me that she and Ron had had sex once, but that it was purely physical. She felt no emotional connection to him.

"Oh," I said, disappointed. "So he's straight, then?"

"Actually, he goes both ways."

"That's cool. I kind of have a crush on him."

"Yeah, Ron is definitely cute, but he's also a bit of a whack-job," she replied.

"How so?" I wondered.

"He lives with this Russian chick named Audrey whom he's been in love with for the past four years. They used to be a couple, but now she despises him. Apparently, he is physically abusive toward her and very possessive."

"Really, Ron?" I couldn't believe what I was hearing. He seemed like such a sweetheart.

"That's the rumor, anyway. She is constantly trash-talking him and she insists that he's a sociopath. She's the one who suggested that he and I sleep together, hoping it would get his mind off her for a while."

I decided to withhold judgment because I know that there are always two sides to every story. Maybe Audrey had some unfounded vendetta against Ron. Maybe she was just jealous that he had more friends than she did or something. Who knew?

A few weeks went by, and I hadn't seen Nicole or Ron around the building at all. Then, one Monday night at 4:00 a.m., there was a loud knock at my door. I awoke, startled. *Who could that be?* I looked through the peephole and I saw Nicole standing out in the hallway, so I opened the door.

"What are you up to?" she asked in a perky tone of voice.

"Well, let's see," I replied sarcastically. "It's a Monday night at 4:00 a.m. and I am currently *off* hard drugs. I'm sleeping! What are *you* doing?"

"Just hanging out. Hey, did you want to buy some shrooms?"

"You mean to tell me that you woke me from a dead sleep at 4:00 a.m. just to sell me psychedelics?" My stern countenance quickly changed to a grin. "Well, why didn't you say so? That's a horse of a different color! C'mon in! Of course I'm interested!"

"I'm glad you stopped using meth," she commented once she was inside the apartment. "You look much better to me now." She then began to complain about her current living situation. She was staying with a friend on the fifth floor who was not a stoner like she was, so they were obviously not compatible as roommates. They argued frequently about issues such as privacy and Nicole's social butterfly lifestyle. I sensed that she needed a change, and since I was pretty bored and lonely at the time myself, I posed the following question:

"How would you feel about moving in with me on a trial basis? My rent is already paid for this month, so I won't even charge you anything to stay here for the rest of the month. If we get along well, we can discuss the possibility of becoming roommates *next* month and sharing the expenses equally." She seemed delighted by the idea.

The next day, Nicole moved in, along with all of her belongings—enough to easily fill the back of a tractor trailer. (O.K., so I'm exaggerating slightly, but only *slightly*, mind you.) As it turned out, we got along great, right from the start. There's something to be said about a woman's touch. She prepared meals for me, helped me decorate my place—quite tastefully—and provided me with good conversation and companionship. Since she knew I was gay, she didn't mind parading around in front of me, naked. We also slept together in the same bed, where we would cuddle sometimes. Other times, we would put on seductive music and light candles while soaking in a hot bubble bath together. It was nice. A little bit *too* nice, I guess, because within a few weeks of her being there, I started to develop intense romantic feelings for her. This surprised me more than it did her, I'm sure. She made me feel like I was a fucking rock star, I swear. She was my Pamela and I felt like Tommy Lee.

How can this be happening to me? I thought to myself. It just didn't make sense. I thought that by this time, at age 34, I knew who I was. Now I was falling for a 21-year-old girl? Perhaps it had something to do with the magic mushrooms we had partaken in together? Anyone who has done shrooms knows that they make you feel especially connected to the earth, to music, to sound and light. Incidentally, we had chosen to ingest the shrooms on November 11, which had been designated as "The National Day of Higher Consciousness." The highest form of consciousness is love, of course, because it clearly states that "God *is* love" in the Bible. With the shrooms acting as a catalyst in my system, had I somehow absorbed this higher consciousness into my own being and then projected those feeling onto her? Or, I wondered, maybe Nicole was some kind of a witch who had cast a spell on me in order to boost her own ego. ("Let's see if I can force a gay man to fall in love with me. That will prove how desirable I truly am . . .") After all, I knew for a fact that she had dabbled in white magic and she was always burning sage and incense. Nothing added up, but all I knew was that I wanted to proclaim my love for her to everyone, from the highest mountain top. Ron in particular was especially excited about the news. Now that I "liked girls," as he put it, he felt more comfortable warming up to me. He tried to act like my "big brother," as he said (even though he is actually five years younger than I am). He was constantly trying to give me advice about women. Ironic, considering the girl he loved wanted nothing to do with him!

"Who knew you were a closet hetero?" he joked.

One night, Ron stopped by to ask me if he could get his motorcycle helmet back. Apparently Nicole had borrowed it for some reason. "Sure," I said. "It's in the closet. Help yourself." Nicole was in the kitchen, preparing dinner. After retrieving his helmet, he bid us goodnight and walked out the door. A few minutes later, he returned. This time, however, he was wearing nothing but a black skull cap. Other than that, he was completely, butt-ass naked. And he looked stunning that way, I must admit.

"You guys mind if I chill here with you for awhile?" he asked me.

Trying my best to disguise my shock, I managed to mutter, "Sure, c'mon in." He proceeded to make small talk with me, as though this were a typical social call, completely disregarding the fact that he was in the buff. Finally, I could no longer contain myself, so I had to say something about it.

"Is there any particular reason you chose to come over here naked?"

"Tomorrow's laundry day," he chuckled. "I couldn't find anything clean to wear, and my work clothes are so binding." Amused by his response, I decided to remove my own clothes. After all, I wanted to be a hospitable host and I thought my guest should be comfortable! So there we were, dicks hanging, while Nicole was concentrating a little *too* hard on the computer screen in front of her. I'm sure she was trying to ignore us because—believe it or not—I had propositioned her that *same day* to participate in a three-way with a cute, 20-year-old Hispanic dude that I had met on the bus.

"I'm relaxed," pressed Ron, "and so is Daniel. Why don't you join us in our nakedness? It's actually quite liberating." Ron, of course, knew nothing about the Hispanic guy, who had left the building about a half hour before Ron showed up nude. What a crazy day. Nicole, however, was less than amused at this point and was unwilling to join in the festivities. (In other words, she was being a total cock-block!) Eventually, Ron sensed her discomfort and decided to go back to his apartment. I was admittedly a little disappointed.

The following day, I offered to take Nicole shopping as sort of an "I'm sorry if I disrespected you in any way yesterday." I certainly never meant to offend her. It's just that I hadn't been with a woman since high school (unless you count those two bisexual films I starred in during the early 2000's). I thought a three-way with another man would be the best way to transition back into it! The funny thing is that I remember really *liking* sex with girls. I'm not sure exactly when or why I decided that I was exclusively "gay," but again I think it all goes back to self-esteem issues. I probably did not think I was "man enough" to attract the type of girl I really wanted. The ole Gay Man's Inferiority Complex reared its ugly head over and over again in my life.

While we were shopping together, Nicole found an adorable orange dress similar in design to the flight attendant outfit that

Britney Spears wears in her *Toxic* video. And it fit her perfectly. She was elated and gracious when I bought it for her, and it felt great seeing her smile and knowing I had brought that smile to her pretty face. It was *not* such a great feeling, however, when she chose to wear the dress out on a date that same night, with another guy. I was crushed. I had asked her to follow *one* simple rule while she was staying there with me for the month: "Please don't invite anyone else to hang out with you here, especially anyone who does not live in this building." Every time I came home from work, I would find her there with another dude. How disrespectful is that? I remember knocking at Ron's door that night, in tears.

"Nicole's young and manipulative," he explained while caressing my shoulders with his fingertips. "She has a lot of intimacy issues. I had sex with her once myself, but I don't have much desire to repeat it. It left me feeling cold and unsatisfied. You don't really need her, dude. If I were you I'd just let her go."

When Nicole returned from her date, she herself seemed less than satisfied with the events of the evening. She told me that the "date" consisted of an awkward sexual episode in which she gave him head and he then promptly drove her back home. I did a cursory scan of her new dress, hoping I wouldn't find any jizz stains on it. She looked irritated and sexually frustrated. Although I was still angry with her, I wanted to somehow ease her pain and help her to relax.

"Please let me make love to you," I begged. "Take my hand and come to the bed with me."

"I don't really know *how* to be made love to," she countered. "I just want to be slapped around." This statement floored me. I had known so many men in my lifetime who viewed sex the same way. It's like they were *ashamed* of their own innate sexual desires, so they felt the subconscious need to be punished or disciplined for their "dirty" thoughts. Was this a result of society and pornography? Or was there something intrinsically unclean about sex itself? Perhaps the act of casual sex reduces us to mere animals running around in heat, with little or no regard for the emotional component that should probably accompany sex between two human beings. I know that it's usually easier for men to separate sex from emotions. Maybe that's why I fell for this girl; she was actually a gay man trapped in a woman's body.

When you think about it, there are very few differences between a man and a dog. The only real difference is that a dog is *honest*. He doesn't pretend to be dedicated to one other dog since dogs have no concept of monogamy. Sexually, a man is similar to a dog because he will lick just about *any* part of the body, especially those parts that emit the strongest pheromones. "Marking" is another term for pissing on someone, just as a dog marks his territory by pissing on a hydrant. (And it's practiced a lot more commonly than I once thought.) Marking gives men a sense of ownership because they leave their scent behind. How completely barbaric! Men in general are often territorial, in or outside of the bedroom.

I had another friend, "Boss," who lived in the building. He was a gang leader. He once told me that if he and I were ever in prison together, I would definitely be his "bitch." Kind of a sweet sentiment, really. See that? Even thugs show their love in some bizarre way. When Boss first moved in, he announced that he had come there to "take over the building." *What an odd thing to say,* I thought. *You are welcome to claim ownership of the building. I have greater aspirations in mind. I am building castles in the sky.* Just as Jesus says, "in my father's house there are many mansions. If it were not so, I would have told you" (John 14:2). I know there is a place being prepared for me, even as I sit here typing this. *Why waste my time with any man other than Jesus?* I've pretty much concluded that men are dogs, and it clearly states in the Bible to not "give that which is sacred to dogs, or cast your *pearls* to *pigs* (Matthew 7:6). Speaking euphemistically, I'm sure most of us know what it means to give someone a "pearl necklace." I think this verse in the Bible is actually implying that random, casual sex reduces us to mere dogs or pigs. I, for one, no longer wish to be in the same category with a pig. Remember my four-day sexcapade? I would *never* consider doing something like that, now that I am clean and sober. Sexual feelings and desires are natural, but we all have to make a conscious decision about the way we choose to handle those desires. I have since decided to save myself for someone who actually *deserves* me. If I never find that person, so be it. (By the way, my most recent HIV test yielded negative results. If that's not an act of God, I don't know what is!)

Was Nicole just another pig? I refused to "slap her around." I was in love with her, for God's sake. I wanted to experience something tender and giving, something completely different from the sadistic sex I'd had with men while high on meth. During gay sex, I often felt like an angry, man-hating dyke with a permanent strap on. While on meth, I would use my dick to take out all my built-up aggressions and frustrations about men in general on the guy I happened to be fucking: "Take it, bitch! This one's for all you douche bags who called me a fag in high school!" One time, in fact, I was slamming it into this one dude, who cried out, "I love having that broad dick in my ass." Not "wide dick," not "fat dick," not "big dick." He said "*broad* dick.*" Broad,* of course, is a slang term for a woman. He somehow knew that I was Venus with a penis, I guess.

Well, getting back to Nicole. I was so disgusted with her that night that I chose not to sleep in the same bed with her. When I returned from work the very next day, all of her things had been removed from my apartment. She had moved back upstairs! I was shocked and devastated. I sat on the sofa and sobbed for hours.

CHAPTER 6

Trouble on the Streets

During the few short weeks that Nicole and I lived together, I had remained meth-free and in high spirits. Her abrupt departure left me, once again, feeling inadequate and terribly depressed. So, not surprisingly, I began to seek out the wonder drug again. This time, I called a contact named Gabriel whose roommate was a dealer. I knew he always had favors to share in exchange for some quality sex. This time, he also had a stash of some very potent GHB (a.k.a. the "date rape drug") which is commonly used in combination with crystal meth during sex. GHB itself is a very dangerous drug because it comes in varied concentrations which cannot be accurately measured or dosed. People often black out (it's known as "crossing over," by the way) for hours, subjecting themselves to physical abuse, rape, or robbery. If you're going to do GHB at all, which I highly suggest *not* doing, it is best to do it while at home and in the company of a trusted companion. I trusted Gabe enough, since I had partied with him several times before and he had been consistently hospitable and friendly. After Gabe and I did our thing, I thanked him and then made the idiotic decision to gulp down a few swigs of the GHB before walking out the door. Huge mistake.

As I was waiting for the bus at about 2:00 a.m., the GHB kicked in full-force and I completely lost my wits. The next thing I remember, I was lying on the ground, completely covered in my own blood, and my wallet and cell phone were gone. At first I thought I had been stabbed or shot, but soon realized that the blood was coming from my nose. Apparently, someone had punched me in the face. In a panic, I staggered to the closest gas station, where the attendant called the police. When they arrived at the scene, I was expecting them to at least give me a ride home and possibly help me recover my missing items. Instead, they treated me like the criminal.

"What in the fuck are you doing out here at this hour, anyway?" barked the angry cop. "I have about two guesses. You are either out here trying to score drugs, or you're here to sell your ass." I was shocked. Aren't the police supposed to "protect and serve?" I assured them that I had been doing nothing of the sort, yet they refused to believe me. They kept repeatedly asking me the same questions over and over again, trying their hardest to catch me in a lie or contradiction.

"I don't remember exactly why I came out tonight," I replied. This was the truth. I guess I was experiencing a form of temporary amnesia as a result of the GHB. Rather than offer any assistance, they half-heartedly wrote up a police report and sent me on my way. Since I had no money to get back home, I had no choice but to just start walking. It was a good 3-4 miles, but I had been known to walk farther distances than that in the past. As I was heading home, I finally remembered the reason I had originally come out that night—to visit Gabriel, who lived just a few blocks from the bus stop where I'd been assaulted.

Looking back, the worst part of that experience was the lack of compassion that I was shown by the other people on the street that night. In fact, several of them chose to add insult and injury to my suffering. A large black woman grabbed me by the hair and pulled me for about two blocks. Another man spat on me. Several others kicked me when I was on the ground. Yet another woman slapped me across the face, causing a wound to tear open directly next to my eyeball with her fingernails. The emotional damage that was incurred that night far outweighed any physical pain I may have been feeling. And, to top it all off, I was solicited for sex by a drunk, 20-something Hispanic kid on the street. *Wow, I must really be hot,* I thought to myself jokingly. *They even want to fuck me when I'm bruised up and covered in blood.*

I eventually found my way back to Gabriel's house. He was there with a new trick from the website, but when he saw my bloody face, he quickly came to my aid and asked his visitor to leave. He helped me recover my phone. We called it and someone answered and agreed to return it. Someone on the street had sold it to him, he said. Gabriel went with me to retrieve the phone, to ensure I would not be put in further danger. Gabe was able to empathize with my plight because he had been through something similar a few years earlier, only he had not fared quite as well as I had. I was left with some scrapes and bruises, but Gabriel had sustained permanent brain damage as a result of his attack. It had clearly been a hate-crime. A group of thugs jumped out of an SUV and cornered him in Weho one night after he left a night club. They ruthlessly struck him in the head with a crowbar, exposing part of his brain. He was left with a permanent dent in his forehead along with random psychotic episodes. At the time of the assault, he did not lose consciousness, miraculously. Rather, he began screaming for help as he tied his t-shirt around his head to act as a tourniquet. His head was gushing with blood like a veritable fountain. When the police arrived, they treated him with total disrespect, exactly as they had treated me. They made no attempt to track down the assholes who had attacked him. They simply blamed him for putting himself in harm's way by being out there at such an ungodly hour. WTF?

My level of respect for the LAPD would soon decline even further with each ensuing encounter with them. They are nothing more than cavemen with billy clubs. I was, however, grateful for the compassion shown to me that night by my angel, Gabriel.

The next day, I called my workplace and notified them about the incident, since I did not want to come to work with my face swollen and be forced to have to explain the situation to every patron and coworker. They advised me to take some time off in order to heal. It was during this period that Ron and I began to bond even further.

Chapter 7

Universal Blossom?

One afternoon, quite unexpectedly, Ron showed up at my door, beaming brightly in that irresistible way of his.

"Hey, do you mind if I crash here for a while? My girl and I aren't getting along at all lately, and I want to give her some space. Besides, I know that you haven't been doing so well since Nicole moved out." He was right. I hadn't been doing well at all, especially considering that I was still in love with her and she was now living with an 18-year-old bisexual named Arnie who lived upstairs. What did she see in *him*, anyway? He was just a skinny kid, really, and had once been a meth addict himself. (A recovered meth addict at 18-years-old? That shows you just how early drug use begins among gay and bisexuals these days!). He also had the very peculiar and self-destructive habit of putting out his cigarettes on the back of his hands. I guess some people would rather feel pain than feel nothing at all. That way, at least they know they are still alive. It wasn't long before Nicole began to imitate him by doing the same thing to her hands.

One time, the four of us (Ron, Nicole, Arnie and I) indulged in a three-day shroom extravaganza which, looking back, was probably one of the best retreats of my life. (Even though it hurt immensely to see Nicole and Arnie playing tonsil hockey like two 8th graders.)

"Don't' worry," Ron comforted me. "Nicole will learn to love you in time."

"Thanks," I grinned half-heartedly, wanting to believe his encouraging words. We then cranked up the retro-pop music, this time Ron and I taking turns as the DJ. I was amazed at how much he and I had in common, as far as our tastes in music were concerned. He knew the words to every song I selected. I felt totally exhilarated as I danced and sang to Paula Abdul's classic, *Straight Up*, while surrounded by my awesome new friends. I was totally present and connected, as though I could have spent the rest of eternity in that moment.

"You're all slaves!" I shouted jubilantly from the rooftop to the city below me.

Things got slightly weirder when Ron led us down to the boiler room in the basement, where he had me lay beside the bubbling well so he could perform some sort of ritualistic baptismal ceremony on me. After chanting an incantation, he pierced my ear (which hurt just a tad) with an earring that he had made himself. It was a dangling yellow mushroom that matched the one he wore around his belt loop. He dubbed the event "Spore Day." He then bestowed a new title upon me: "Universal Blossom." At the time, I wasn't quite sure what he meant by that. Was it supposed to mean that I was a universally appealing "flower" to all men, despite their sexual identities? Ron identified as heterosexual, even though he had admitted to having had gay experiences in the past. He also complimented me on what a "nice cock" I had that day he came over naked to my apartment. Or did "Universal Blossom" mean something deeper? Was I the blossom who held the power and wisdom to "seed" the next level of the species in human evolution? Either way, it was a pretty cool title.

Of course, I was thrilled at the idea of living with Ron. Sometimes we would cuddle together on the bed, which was nice. The best part, though, was the way we transformed my apartment into a virtual nightclub complete with flashing lights, a killer sound system, and eye-catching decorations of every kind. It was pretty much a non-stop, 24-hour party. Ron was often strung-out on his usual combination of valium and ephedrine, and sometimes I would find him asleep on the toilet or in the closet, which alarmed me. He never wanted the party to stop, so sometimes he would just fall asleep wherever he happened to be, like a narcoleptic. I remember helping him tie his necktie for a business luncheon one morning after he we had stayed up all night rocking out to electro-pop music together.

"I'm so lucky," he said sweetly. "Every day you grow more and more beautiful in my eyes." *Uh-oh*, I thought to myself. *I think I might be falling in love, again.* I was becoming quickly attached to him, just as I had become attached to Nicole. They were both easy to live with (there was never an argument) and having a companion really did prevent me from looking for meth—which is what I always wound up doing when I was bored and lonely. The trouble with Ron, of course, was that he was unwilling to admit to himself that he had any homosexual feelings, even though I had personally seen him make out with Arnie once.

"It doesn't mean anything," insisted Ron. That line of reasoning made no sense to me at all. Sure, I could understand having my dick sucked by a random dude and it not meaning anything, but to actually kiss someone one the *mouth?* That was a little too personal to dismiss as simple fun and games. Hadn't Ron seen *Pretty Woman?* Clearly, he had issues.

The most outlandish, hair-brained idea that Ron ever had was to build a hot tub in the boiler room one night. We used a hose to siphon the warm well water into a giant plastic tarp, which we suspended around a frame made of chairs, plywood, or whatever else we could find. Had the tarp given out, we could have easily been electrocuted, since the boiler room was filled with electrical fuse boxes. But no risk, no glory, right? Living with Ron was like enjoying a second childhood all over again. That is, until it all came crashing down . . .

CHAPTER 8

Boys Will Be Boys

It all started one night while Ron was away, presumably at one of his "party till dawn" raves. Feeling bored and restless, I logged onto my usual website and within minutes found someone with party favors to share. I hopped on the bus toward Weho, where I eventually got my fix. After leaving the guy's place, I decided to stop at the 24-hour IHOP to use the bathroom (FYI: meth is a diuretic and it makes you urinate, a *lot*). Anyway, I pushed the door open to the men's room, which was unlocked, to find two thuggish young black men inside the bathroom.

"Sorry," I stammered meekly as I closed the door to wait my turn outside the bathroom. The door immediately swung open again.

"What the fuck are you doing, punk?" one of them asked me in a nasty tone of voice. "Get in here." They then forced me to my knees onto the floor in a puddle of urine next to the toilet. They pulled out their enormous, semi-erect dicks and ordered me to "Suck them, bitch." Half afraid and half-aroused (I *was* still high, after all), I politely declined and refused to open my mouth. "We know that's what you want," they sneered as they zipped up their jeans and gave each other a high-five. They left the bathroom, laughing. When I finished using the bathroom, I entered the dining area of the restaurant and spotted the two of them sitting at a table with two girls (possibly their girlfriends?). Never one to tolerate disrespect, I marched up to the table and confronted them.

"Do you mind telling me what that was all about?" I asked, annoyed.

"What's he talking about?" asked one of the young ladies at the table.

"Should I tell them?"

They both shook their heads and shifted their eyes as if to say "No, please, don't." (Who's in control of the situation *now*, bitches?)

"There is never a reason to treat someone that way," I continued. "We all have our issues, but you ought to consider that maybe I am not the type of person you may assume to me be. Maybe the idea of being "forced" to do something is what compels us to do things we wouldn't otherwise do."

"No disrespect meant," one of them stammered. I left the restaurant, feeling a bit shaken and more than a bit self-justified. Who did these people think they were, anyway?

As I was walking toward the bus stop, I noticed a 21-year-old man named Jake whom I'd met once before at a drug dealer's apartment. He and I had hit if off the very first time we met. I had never believed in love at first sight before, but I was instantly drawn to him. Nicole had given me an Ed Hardy hat, which I adored and wore every day. It was designed with a skull and roses with a caption that read, "Love Kills Slowly." Oddly enough, Jake wore a pair of sneakers with the *exact* same design on them. How cute. Apparently, Jake had moved to L.A. from the South last May, just as I had done. Although he originally had come for spring break, he quickly got caught up in the drug scene and never returned home. He was amazingly talented, musically. He could free-style like no one I'd ever heard, and he would spit rapid-fire verses that rang with truth, soul, and passion.

"I *am* music," he told me the first time we met. It had always been my personal philosophy that God and music are synonymous and indivisible—that music is the closest thing we have to a physical manifestation of God in the material world. Together, Jake and I sang the chorus to *Hard Out There for a Pimp*, from the bad-ass movie, *Hustle and Flow*. Although Jake had a hardened look about him, he also maintained a childlike innocence and beauty at the same time (not to mention a washboard stomach and a great sense of fashion). He was a little bit street and a little bit sweet. The first time I met him, he told me he was homeless. I was surprised to hear that, considering how good he looked, physically. As we were reunited, I told him about the incident at IHOP, as well as the catastrophe that occurred when I had been mugged on Santa Monica Blvd.

"People are horrible," he said disdainfully. "That kinda shit wouldn't happen to you if you had a big bro like me around to protect you." I melted. Did this beautiful young man really care about me? Was there actually hope for humanity, after all? He then asked me if I "partied."

"Yeah," I replied.

"I have some," he said. "You have a place we can chill?" Needless to say, I welcomed him into my apartment. And, just as homeless Joe had suddenly turned into a demon upon entering my place, Jake began acting very strangely the moment he walked into the room. The first thing he did was tear down my Michael Jackson poster that was hanging on my wall, and then he found and destroyed the Bible that the angel had given me on the airplane.

"The Bible is useless drivel," he said. "It was written by Shakespeare and has no historical or spiritual relevance to real life. Even Jesus himself says *do not worship me*." Jake had some sort of Messiah complex, apparently. He literally believed that he was God and was always trying to convince me, through trickery, into believing the same thing. Sometimes, I actually allowed myself to believe his deceitful words. I probably should have asked him to leave right then, but I was entirely too smitten to realize just how disrespectful he was behaving. He then ordered me to "drink this," a bottle of Gatorade or something that Ron had specifically asked me to *not* drink (he even taped the words, "DO NOT DRINK" to it, which Jake apparently removed). Without thinking, I drank it. He then showed me the scars on his leg, which looked like hundreds of tiny slash marks. Each one represented someone he had murdered, he told me. He later laughed it off as a joke. I, for one, thought he would say or do just about anything to come across as being tougher than he actually was.

Jake found a pair of Ron's sunglasses, and as he put them on, he stated that "The music brought me back to life." It was at that moment that I realized something incredible: Jake, with the sunglasses on, looked *exactly* like Grant. Jake was white and Native American and Grant had been a very light-skinned black guy, but the resemblance was uncanny. If I had snapped a photo of Jake in those red sunglasses and sent it to Grant's mother, I'm sure she would have thought it was her late son. How had I not noticed the resemblance until now? *Had the music really brought Grant back from the dead?* I had spent countless nights alone in my room, dancing and singing in worship to the Lord, asking him to bring my Grant back to me. Jesus does say that "*Anything* you ask in my name shall be granted unto you," and that with God all things are within the realm of reason (John 14:14). After all, it worked for Lazarus, so why couldn't it work for Grant? Had my faith and undying hope finally paid off?

I was also struck by how similar Jake's dancing style was to that of my own. It was as though we shared the same spirit. A photographer who lived downstairs from me had taken some photos of me "shadow dancing" in my apartment. As I temporarily froze my body into various poses, he would snap photos of me and my shadow as it was cast onto the wall. While Jake danced, I watched his shadow. It was as though I were seeing the same photos of myself all over again. I was ecstatic and overwhelmed. I wanted everyone (Nicole, Arnie, and Ron) to meet this amazing man, to hear his music and feel his energy. My Grant had been brought back from the dead!

Nicole was not interested. When I asked her to come downstairs to meet him, she pulled out the Bible and read me the verse about "wolves in sheep's clothing" and false prophets. Jesus *does* say that many men will come in his name, but if anyone claims to be him, "I assure you that he is not" (Matthew 24:5).

So I called Ron, who was at work, and explained to him that I had met a new friend who would be staying with us for awhile. "I just wanted to clear it with you, first," I told Ron over the phone. "He's an amazingly gifted man who just needs a place to stay right now. He also told me that he is in negotiations to be signed with Def Jam Records! You have to hear him free-style."

"It's your place, dude," Ron replied. "Whatever you wanna do is cool with me."

A few minutes later, my phone rang. It was Ron again, but this time his voice sounded more urgent. "Daniel, I was just in a motorcycle accident."

"Oh, no!" I exclaimed. "Are you hurt?"

"No, I just have a few scrapes on my hands and arms."

"Is your bike totaled?"

"No, it just has a few little scratches on it that can easily be fixed." Ron, incidentally, was known as "Mr. Fix-it," the resident handy-man.

"Oh, OK, cool then. I'm glad you are OK."

"Thanks," he said. "Hey, I am going to stop by the apartment for a few minutes in order to dress these wounds before heading back to work for the day. I will see you shortly."

About twenty minutes later, Ron burst through the door. He glanced up and down at Jake, then at the apartment, which was in complete disarray.

"Empty your pockets," he ordered Jake.

"Ron!" I shouted. "What are you doing? Jake has been with me the whole time. He wouldn't steal from us."

"I *said*, empty your pockets," he repeated impatiently.

"Did you want to take this outside?" Jake countered.

"Take off my sunglasses. For fuck's sake, you broke them! These cost me 350 bucks!" shouted Ron. *What a coincidence,* I thought. *That's the exact amount of money you promised to pay me in rent for the month.* I guarantee there is no way in *hell* that a pair of red plastic sunglasses cost him more than ten dollars.

"Stop it, both of you!" I cried. Unbelievable! Two straight guys fighting over me? I had seen it all.

"Either you leave now, or I'm calling the cops," retorted Ron.

Damn, this guy had nerve! It *was*, after all, my apartment. Ron had not paid me a cent to stay there, so far.

"Fine, I'm outta here," replied Jake, who more than likely had warrants out for his arrest and wanted nothing to do with the cops. Jake then asked me to join him for lunch somewhere.

"Daniel's not going anywhere," Ron yelled. "I'm telling you one more time to leave, now!"

When I tried to follow Jake out the door, Ron attacked me and pinned me down on the bed with all of his strength. "Get the fuck off me, Ron!" I screamed at the top of my lungs until my voice was hoarse. A few moments later, Audrey and her friend, Mark, entered the apartment, breaking up the commotion.

"I was injured in a bike accident and all you can talk about is how great this other guy is," snapped Ron. "I'm not gonna let you ruin your life by chasing after that tweaker. And he was destroying all of our stuff! The apartment looks like shit."

"It's *my* life!" I shouted. "And I asked you if you were hurt in the accident and you said no! I'm sorry if poor little Ron isn't getting enough attention!" Clearly, Ron was just jealous of Jake and felt threatened by Jake's swag and physical attractiveness. Looking back, Ron and Jake were actually a lot alike. They both wanted someone who would worship *him*. The earring Ron gave me was a sign of ownership; he wanted to make me into his minion. Unfortunately, that's the typical man's mindset. He wants a spouse and/or kids who will look to him as a pillar of strength and wisdom. He needs to feel like a god as a means of building up that ego of his. The ego (the *false* self) is, by definition, fragile; it constantly craves reinforcement and often feels threatened. Truthfully, if Ron had wanted to be with me, he could have easily had me. But he claimed that he wasn't interested in men, remember? Was I supposed to just wait around until he came to terms with his sexuality? I could have been waiting for the rest of my life, on *his* terms.

"You don't want me, Ron, but you don't want anybody else to have me, either! Just get the fuck out of my life."

So that was that. He gathered up his precious belongings (I swear, material things were more valuable to him than people's feelings were) and left. I was completely devastated. A few hours ago, I had been living out a fantasy lifestyle of my own making. I was living with two super-cuties (whom I didn't even have to put out for) in a non-stop atmosphere of music and partying. Then, within a blink of an eye, it was all taken away from me. Ron had pulled the tablecloth right out from under my royal feast. I had no way of contacting Jake, either, because he didn't have a cell phone. Yet again, I was left alone in my apartment, sobbing.

The next day, I passed Ron in the hallway. He was already wearing a new pair of sunglasses identical to the ones Jake had supposedly broken. I asked him about the rent money he had promised me. There was something different about Ron, today. It looked as though he had snapped.

"I'm not giving you anything!" he screeched. "You're little friend damaged my property and I'm holding you accountable."

"But you gave me your word!" I said. "How am I supposed to make rent this month?"

"Give them half of what you owe, and then pay the other half later. I do it all the time. In fact, I'm doing it this month." So the truth was, he didn't *have* the money he owed me; it had nothing to do with Jake or the broken sunglasses. "Does that make sense, bitch, or do I have to pound it through your skull with my fist?" he shouted. I couldn't believe this was coming from the same Ron who was always going around saying "peace and love" all the time. Did he even know what those things meant?

Audrey had been right all along, and I should have listened to her. "Everything he does comes at a price," she once warned me. "He makes it seem as though he's doing something for you, but everything he does is for himself."

I tore off the earring he had made me and threw it to the floor, crushing it with my foot. Then he had the audacity to ask me if I had had sex with Jake (as if it were any of his goddamn business!).

"It wasn't about sex," I told him. "That's not why I was in it with you, and that's not why I wanted to be in it with Jake, either." I wanted a bromance, not a romance. I swear, men just don't understand what love is.

Chapter 9

My Christmas Gift

Ron always parked his motorcycle in the same spot, so I could see it from my kitchen window and know he was home. *Talk about eels on wheels*, I joked to myself.

As the weeks continued, my anger toward Ron began to subside a bit. All of the drama with Jake prompted me to embark on yet another sobriety spell, and for once I actually started to feel in good spirits while remaining sober and alone! Christmas was approaching; maybe I was feeling the Christmas spirit? I decided to make amends with Ron. I sent him a text that said, "Should I ask Santa for my friend back? It's Christmas, for Christ's sake, Ron! Can't we just forget all this foolishness?"

His response: "Perhaps Santa should have a talk with the landlord. I am being evicted from the building for breaking into the boiler room."

I'm not sure how the landlord found out about our adventures down in the boiler room; I had certainly never mentioned it to him. In any event, I tried to clear Ron's name with the landlord, but to no avail.

"Ron's not a bad *neighbor*," I told the landlord. "I just wouldn't recommend living with him on a domestic level. To my knowledge, he has not done anything too insidious around here. He just likes to be adventurous, like in the *Goonies*. He's like a little kid in that way."

"Tell Ron that if he has a problem with the decision, he can talk to me himself. There are restricted areas of the building for a *reason*. He is putting himself and other tenants in physical danger by breaking the rules here, and I don't need that kind of liability. I will be the one who is held responsible in the end for any damages he does to the building."

Ron was getting just what he deserved. He kept offering to fix my earring for me, which I refused to allow him to do. Did he honestly think I was still in love with him?

"I'm thinking of getting a dangling crucifix to replace the mushroom," I told Ron. After all, I wasn't Ron's bitch. I belong to nobody but Jesus.

With Ron out of the picture and Jake nowhere to be found, I began to fixate on Nicole again, believe it or not! I went out and bought her a lovely charm bracelet as a Christmas gift. Still, I felt kind of bad trying to court her because I knew she did not return my feelings. I'm also sure she loved to be lavished with gifts and attention, and she used me more than a few times to make Arnie jealous since he was the non-commitment type (aren't *all* 18-year-old boys the non-commitment type, though?) Her attempts to get a rise out of Arnie were apparently working, though. One time, Arnie and I bumped into each other at Boss' place. Boss had a sword hanging on his wall, which Arnie removed from the wall and examined carefully.

"Wow, this is real sword," he said, impressed. "You mean I could use this thing to kill someone?" he said, while glaring at me. At first I thought he was joking, but it soon become clear to me that he was not kidding at all. He pointed the sword directly at me. He then made a swift motion with the sword across his own neck, all the while looking at me with his best "stay away from my girl" look in his eyes. Shortly after that, he started this ridiculous rumor in the building that I was a vampire.

"How do you think he stays so young-looking? He's practically 35-years-old and he looks younger than I do! Vampires can't age," I overheard him whispering to Nicole one afternoon. Pretty soon, he began recruiting other tenants to join his vampire-slaying squad. As if I weren't paranoid enough as it was, I now had half of the building conspiring against me. Maybe they were just trying to harass me, but you have to remember, I was on meth at the time. What may have been fun and games for them became yet another reason to keep me in a state of fear. So I kept a low profile. I stayed away from everyone.

I was starting to feel pretty damn good about everything until Christmas Eve finally arrived, when I was haunted by memories of Grant's death. Remember, he had died less than two weeks before Christmas. My family was on the other side of the country. Tim barely spoke to me and never visited me (besides, he always traveled home to Pittsburgh for the holidays, anyway). I was faced with the reality that I would be spending Christmas completely alone.

Wallowing in my own self-pity, I ventured into Weho on Christmas Eve. At precisely five minutes before midnight, I said a very tearful prayer to Jesus: "Please bring my Grant back," I pleaded. "I am so tired of feeling alone and being taken advantage of. Surely, there must be a way for me to experience love again in my life." Then, five minutes later, at exactly midnight, I saw Jake walk right past me on the sidewalk. I was elated. *Wow*, I thought. *You are really on the ball tonight, God!*

He instantly recognized me and I apologized profusely for Ron's behavior. I explained that I had thrown Ron out that very day because of the way he had treated him.

"No worries, my friend," Jake smiled. "Ron was probably just trying to protect you, the same way I want to offer you protection. Besides, it's our birthday today! Happy Birthday." It's odd that he said that to me, especially considering the fact that one of my neighbors had just given me some frankincense as a Christmas gift.

"Isn't that one of the gifts they gave Him?" he asked me upon presenting me with the frankincense.

Jake handed me a small package containing, you got it, crystal meth. Then he started ranting and raving about some elusive castle in the Hollywood Hills, where his "sister," Lady Gaga, lived. According to him, she wanted him to bring me back to the castle so she could have sex with me. To this day, I am not sure whether he was kidding or just strung-out and delusional. Either way, I had my Grant back. I didn't care if he thought he lived on Pluto! Actually, when I first met him, he did mention that he was "from another planet."

"You are the only person Lady Gaga wants to fuck," Jake told me. I took this as a huge compliment, considering that Lady Gaga has publicly declared her lack of interest in sex, specifically casual sex. I think it was Jake's way of letting me know that I was the only person *he* wanted to fuck (even though he, like Ron, identified as heterosexual). I was like a magnet for these types of men in denial! Although my curiosity about Gaga's castle was piqued, I decided it was probably a better idea to just go back to my place instead. I had a stash of fresh shrooms saved up just for the occasion. I wouldn't be spending Christmas alone, after all! Jake was my unexpected Christmas gift.

While we were tripping on the shrooms, we could not stop laughing. We just sat there, staring at each other for hours, giggling with delight like two twelve-year-old girls. "This must be what heaven is like," I told him. "Never-ending happiness without needing to really do any type of activity to keep us entertained." The unspoken love between us was all we needed.

"It's like I can see right through you," Jake cooed. "Are you a virgin?"

I was struck by this question, considering that I had probably had more sexual partners in my lifetime than Jenna Jamison had. What Jake was seeing, I'm sure, was the purity of my heart. As it says in the Bible, "Blessed are the pure of heart, for they shall see God (Matthew 5:8)." Although I had rented out my body to hundreds of men in exchange for money or drugs, I had never given *myself* to any of them. For this reason, I considered myself to be a "Virgin Whore" similar to Mary Magdalene, betrothed to Christ.

Jake confessed to me that he was not interested in sex—that he was "saving" himself for his one true love: Miley Cyrus. His favorite TV show was *Hanna Montana, Pop Princess* and he had all of Miley's albums and knew every lyric to every one of her songs. I found this to be hysterically funny, since he also tried to come across as a bad-ass thug to everyone. Show me another gangsta who listens to Miley Cyrus, please! I had the sneaking suspicion that he didn't really want to have sex with Miley Cyrus, either—simply because I knew she was a female! Ms. Cyrus was to Jake exactly what Paula Abdul had always been to me. He didn't want to *fuck* Miley Cyrus; he wanted to *be* Miley Cyrus.

According to Jake, he had once disguised himself as an "ugly clown" a few years ago. He intentionally made himself as ugly as possible using make-up and unappealing clothing. He claimed that while he was dressed as the ugly clown, he met Miley Cyrus in a restaurant and she told him that he was beautiful.

"She was the only person to see through my disguise," he said. I found that story to be absolutely endearing. We all wear our own "disguises" in life. Nobody wants to completely reveal their true selves because they are *afraid* of being rejected on some level. But, just as Miley Cyrus had seen the real Jake in spite of his costume, Jake was able to see the real, pure *me*. He was not judging me as the old hag on the bus had done. That is why Jesus says "it is children like these" who will inherit the kingdom of heaven (Matthew 19:14). Young children are very often drawn to me instantly, because they do not judge. No three-year-old boy looks at me and thinks, "He's probably gay" or "he looks like a tweaker." Children look past the exterior and they, like God, see only what's in the *heart*.

As we continued to trip harder on the shrooms, Jake started referring to me as "Miley Cyrus." I'm not sure whether his drug-induced mind was playing tricks on him or whether he just wanted an excuse to seduce me. Either way, he kept exposing his gigantic, erect cock and begging me to perform oral sex on him. Now, I have seen more than my share of dicks in my lifetime, so it takes a lot to impress me. Still, I have to admit, I was impressed with this one! I avoided blowing him, though, because I was uncomfortable with the idea that he might *actually* think I was Miley Cyrus. I wanted him to want me for *me*, rather than help him play out his fantasies about Miley Cyrus. So instead, we just went to bed together, naked, and fell asleep in each others arms. We had the stereo playing softly in the background. Nat King Cole's classic song, *Unforgettable*, began to play.

"Remember when we wrote this song together?" Jake asked me, just before he drifted off into dreamland. I stopped for a moment and pondered this thought. Who's to say that we hadn't written that song together in some other lifetime, in some other form?

Chapter 10

Jake the Snake?

The next day, Arnie stopped by to apologize for the sword incident. "I'm sorry about everything," he said. "I don't really think you're a vampire. Besides, Nicole and I broke up a few days ago. She was driving me crazy with all her neediness."

I introduced him to Jake. I thought I noticed a bit of flirtation between the two of them, which at the time caused me to seethe with jealousy inside. (Jake even referred to Arnie as "Miley Cyrus" at least once!) Intrigued by Jake, Arnie agreed to smoke the "peace pipe" with us, despite having been vehemently anti-meth in the past. I'm pretty sure he was hoping for a three-way. Since he and Nicole had just broken up, she was no longer living with him. He was probably having a moment of weakness, which is why he chose to partake in the crystal meth we offered him.

Arnie was a very gifted psychic medium, and people of all ages and walks would come to him for tarot readings, palm readings, etc. While he was visiting me that day, I asked him to perform a reading for me regarding my new friendship with Jake. Could I really trust this guy? Was he a friend or a foe? The cards revealed that Jake was not only a friend, but a potential lover as well.

"The love card is extremely rare and very important," Arnie explained to me. "Even Nicole and I did not get the love card when I did a reading for the two of us." The cards also showed that I represented *temperance*. There was that word again! Remember, it was written on Grant's belt buckle the day he died.

"Your responsibility is to help Jake get in touch with his feminine energy. Only then can the two of you experience love," Arnie told me. Arnie also bestowed a new name upon Jake. "I want to call you *Marcel*," Arnie declared. "It means *from the sea.*"

"That's correct," verified Jake. "I come from the sea." Jake then showed us a spooky video clip of himself he had posted online. In the video, he used flashing lights and shadows to create the effect of himself crawling out of the depths of darkness—pushing his way to the surface and breaking free. His mouth was covered in red make-up to symbolize blood lust. While watching the video, I recalled that in the book of Revelation, it says that the antichrist will rise up "out of the sea" (Rev. 13:1).

The next day, Nicole dropped by. I'm sure she had caught wind of my new houseguest, whom she originally refused to meet.

"What's up?" I asked her.

"Would you guys mind if I stayed here with you for a while? The break-up with Arnie has been really hard on me. I still love him but we just can't seem to get along."

I still had feelings for her, so I couldn't possibly say no, and she knew it. As it turned out, she was just using me in order to get with Jake. *This chick has some nerve,* I thought to myself. She would literally throw herself at Jake, right in front of me. She was exactly Andy Warhol's definition of a *cunt:* "A *whore* is someone who will sleep with *anyone,*" Warhol once said. "A *cunt* is someone who will sleep with anyone but *you."* She had moved out the first time because she felt that I had somehow disrespected her, yet she had no problem stripping in front of me and desperately wrapping her naked body around Jake like a starfish. I actually didn't mind though, since I found the entire situation to be rather titillating. The three of us slept in the same bed, with Nicole in the middle. She would practically *beg* him to fuck her with that monster dick of his, but he clearly had no interest in doing so. He would just lay there and masturbate, all the while staring at *me.* I recall the time I wrapped the Christmas charm bracelet I had bought for Nicole around my dick while Jake watched me jerk off, mesmerized. Yet he still insisted that he wasn't gay at all. Give me a friggin break, dude!

Jake kept referring to Nicole as "the maid," since she walked around the apartment in a catatonic trance, cleaning and reorganizing everything yet never making a sound. It was as though she had been hypnotized into being our personal servant. After a few days, she finally began to realize that Jake had zero interest in her, so she moved back in with her brother. This time, however, I was not all that upset about her decision to leave. Clearly, she had been taking advantage of me, yet again.

I never so much as asked either Nicole or Jake for a single dime, yet neither one of them seemed the least bit gracious toward me. Jake made no effort whatsoever to help me clean up the apartment. In fact, he was always creating messes for me to clean up. He never lifted a finger to even wash a dish, and he ate more food in a day than Michael Phelps would have.

But we did enjoy each other's company. He would free-verse and I would dance. Together we would "call the corners." One time, in particular, we video-taped one of our jam sessions and when we watched it back on the monitor, the images were astonishing. There were two ethereal beings caught on camera. One looked like a dark lord whose shadow was cast upon the wall. He was mouthing the words as Jake rapped. The other was a face identical to that of my own, floating above Jake near the ceiling all in white light. Most of Jake's music was dark and foreboding. He viewed himself as a vigilante of sorts, specifically against child molesters. Hateful words of vengeance spilled from his lips, cursing child molesters and sentencing them to eternal damnation.

He eventually admitted to me that he had been sexually abused as a child, which explains why he tore down my Michael Jackson poster that day. Personally, I do not believe the allegations against Michael Jackson. He was a gentle, child-like creature himself—I refuse to believe that he could possibly be capable of such depravity. And besides, nobody but God knows the truth, so why not give the guy the benefit of the doubt?

"It's not your responsibility to rid the world of evil," I told Jake, my eyes welling up with tears. "God has appointed Satan as the guardian of hell; let Satan do his job. I'm so sorry that happened to you, baby, but it's the *past*. You have to let it go! Why focus on the negative past when you can spread love instead of animosity? After all, what in this world *really* matters?"

"Nothing." After he spoke that one word, Jake convulsed violently and vomited green bile everywhere. It was as though an exorcism had taken place—a healing from within Jake's very soul. He starting free-styling again, but this time he spoke promising words of hope, optimism, and humanity. It was the best material I had ever heard from him. Had he been delivered from his painful past? Was there a chance that he could forgive his molester and finally come to terms with his sexuality, rather than fight it or blame it on his unfortunate childhood abuse? I noticed a drastic, positive change within Jake that occurred almost instantly, or so I thought.

A few days later, while we were high on meth, Jake physically transformed into Grant, right before my eyes. It wasn't just his appearance, either. It was his movements, his mannerisms, his expressions.

"Grant?" I muttered, in disbelief. Jake simply nodded his head, *yes*. "But how?"

Jake then pointed to the tattoo of the cross on his right arm.

"Jesus?"

Again, he nodded silently. I was stunned and amazed. Had Grant and I actually conquered physical death through our belief in Christ? Would there be no more suffering and pain in my life? Just as I was actually beginning to believe that we had overcome death, Jake ignited the burners on my gas range and then inserted a metal screwdriver into the burning flame.

"Let me give you a mark on your hand," he said. My mood quickly changed from overjoyed to enraged. In the book of Revelation, it states that the antichrist and those who follow him will be "branded with a mark on the forehead or the right hand" (Rev. 14:9). It also prophesizes about a "false *resurrection*" that could even fool, if possible, the elect (God's chosen ones). Had Jake been sent as a trickster, using the name of Jesus to try to separate me from God? I immediately ordered him to turn off the burners and leave my house.

"Even if you *are* Grant, to hell with both of you!" I said to Jake. He reacted violently, insisting that I was an ingrate who should be thanking him. Thanking him? He was just someone I had met on the street. I had brought him into my home and had shared everything with him and asked him for nothing. He should have been thanking me!

"Who died for your sins?" he asked me.

"Jesus."

"You're welcome," he said emphatically.

"You aren't Jesus," I rebuked him.

"How do you know?" he questioned me.

"Because you *aren't.*" I know for certain that it says in the Bible that you will be able to distinguish "false prophets" from true prophets based upon the fruits of the spirit—patience, joy, love, kindness, *temperance*, gentleness, meekness (Galatians 5:22-23). Even now, Jake was enraged and bitter, and had always been greedy, impatient, gluttonous, and self-serving. Remember the seven deadly sins? Jake was the personification of just about all of them! "I suggest you leave now, before I have to have Boss take care of matters for me."

Within minutes, Jake was gone. He and Boss were actually rival gang members and he wanted no trouble with Boss. The last thing he said to me was, "I'll see you ate the gates." Creepy!

So, there I was once again, alone and very confused. Had I done the right thing? If God loves his children unconditionally, then why could I not find it in my heart to forgive Jake? I decided to seek the advice of others. I ventured out into Hollywood, where I met three people sitting at a table in a nightclub.

"If you were *happily* married and then found out that your spouse was the antichrist, would you want a divorce?" I asked them. I received mixed responses to the question, but I remember one of the women laughing and saying, "No way. If you're happy, then you're happy. My husband *is* the antichrist."

Just then, one of my favorite Mariah Carey songs, *Touch my Body*, started playing loudly at the club. Instinctively, I started to move seductively along with the music. A bouncer immediately approached me and insisted that I leave the premises.

"Why?" I asked, startled.

"Because you don't have a drink in your hand."

"I haven't had the chance to approach the bar, yet," I explained.

"I don't care," he snapped. "Either you leave now, or I will be forced to remove you, physically." I was outraged. Clearly, my dancing had offended him because it aroused him sexually and he could not deal with those feelings within himself. I probably should have just moved on to another club, but I did not appreciate the disrespect or the discrimination. I wasn't hurting anyone, and it was a *dance* club, for the love of God! I certainly was not the only person there without a drink in my hand, either. I was sick and tired of letting assholes like him walk all over me. I know that Jesus says to "turn the other cheek," but I only had so many cheeks, and by this time all of them were sore.

"I'm not going anywhere," I said as I stood firmly on my two feet.

He grabbed my arm and forcefully tried to pull me toward the door, but I could not be budged. Within minutes my arm was scraped and bleeding, but I still refused to leave. He called the police, of course. When they arrived, he told them that I had been harassing guests and "exposing myself" to patrons. I was livid. What gave this man the right to bear false witness against me? I had done no such thing! Luckily, there was a surveillance camera which the police reviewed, and of course there was no evidence of me doing anything remotely inappropriate (much to their disappointment, I'm sure). As usual, the cops sided with the bouncer and treated me with total disdain.

"You're going to have to find another night club tonight," they ordered me coldly. "I'm not gonna stand here all night and play these games with you." Obviously, I wasn't the one who was playing games. I was no longer in the mood to party, as I'm sure you can imagine, so I just went back home.

Was Jake actually the antichrist? Or was he just temporarily possessed because of the meth? He had, on more than one occasion, referred to himself as a "shape-shifter," or the "red dragon." (A "shape-shifter" is an alien who has the power to assume other forms, often taking the shape of a human being in order to disguise itself.) Had he come from the reptilian race beneath the earth's surface in order to lead me astray? As it says in the Bible, such deceitful men will come during the end times, appearing "godly in form" but being "lovers of themselves" (2 Tim 3:1-5). This described Jake to an absolute T! According to the Bible, these men will lead *foolish* women astray—keeping these women in a state of "always learning but never *knowing*" the truth (2 Timothy 7). Was Jake, quite literally, just a cold-hearted snake? I deserved somebody better, girl, and I was not about to play the *fool* now.

I started to worry that maybe Jake really was part of the infamous *Illuminati*, and I began to see signs of the beast everywhere I turned. I saw dragons in the clouds and snake imprints on the ground. Reptiles of every kind appeared everywhere I looked. Were my own fears causing me to hallucinate?

I remember meeting a photographer who did a photo-shoot of me. Clearly, in several of the pictures, I saw an alien presence surrounding me, wrapping its tentacles around my body. When I pointed out the aliens to the photographer, he hastily ripped up the photos because he was unable to accept the truth; he was in denial. Either that, or he already *knew* something and was trying to destroy the evidence by tearing up the photos. This is the time I began to see myself as the Alien Princess, who was trapped in a tower (this world) that was guarded by a dragon (the Unholy Spirit/evil). A week or so after that, I dropped in, unannounced, on the same photographer. One of the photos he had taken of me happened to be lying on his bed when I walked into his bedroom. It was a shot of just my torso, and I noticed that he had blown up the photo and painted it blue and green, like the Earth. He also had smeared his own blood around the perimeter of the photo and entitled it "Blood from a Stone." Was he working directly for the Dark Forces, as well? Were they trying to somehow destroy me, despite my loyalties to Christ? Would I be able to remain grounded with my own soul safely intact it its original body?

When I returned home, they were busy filming a high-budget movie on the first floor of the building where I lived. I recall approaching one of the crew members.

"Excuse me," I said. "This film wouldn't happen to be about an alien princess who is trapped in a tower that's guarded by a dragon, would it?"

"No," she chuckled. "We did that one yesterday. This one's about a young man who is having some problems with his life."

"Gee," I responded sarcastically. "I don't know anybody like *that*, do you?"

"No, not personally," she smirked before turning away from me.

Chapter 11

Angels and Aliens

Things just kept getter weirder by the day. For example, I once mopped my kitchen floor and ten minutes later, I found the mop broken in half. The wooden pieces from the mop's handle were arranged like a pair of crossbones. A tiny black devil's horn was stapled to the top of one of the wooden sticks. I didn't even own a stapler! Another time, I was sitting at my computer desk when I heard the distinct sound of knocking coming from inside a sealed cabinet in my kitchen (the cabinet had once been a pull-out ironing board). Trembling in terror, I slowly approached the sealed cabinet and knocked loudly three times in response. The knocking sound coming from the other side immediately ceased. Yet another time, I found a pair of red leather knuckle gloves that Ron had given me. They were folded and shaped into faces that looked exactly like a goat's face. I flattened the gloves out to their normal position, only to find them once again contorted to look like the goat the very next day. Was the devil himself behind these phenomena, or were my own *fears* creating these realities, right before my eyes?

I tried to relax by sunbathing on the rooftop. As I lay there, gazing at the clear blue sky, I saw two birds circling around each other, ascending higher and higher into the stratosphere until they were barely visible to the naked eye. *That's strange,* I thought. *I've never seen a bird fly that high before.* Suddenly, they transformed into beams of light and instantly shot across the horizon. Maybe these weren't birds at all, but some sort of alien surveillance devices? I had just heard on the news a few days before about a mysterious episode in which hundreds of birds had suddenly died while in flight, falling to the ground. Maybe, I thought, that once the aliens finished using the birds for their own invasive purposes, the "birds" simply malfunctioned and expired.

Then, I began to see millions of black, snakelike creatures descending from the sky. All of them appeared to be covered in suction cups along their coiled bodies. It reminded me of a dream I once had, years ago, about microscopic celestial parasites that fell to the earth, contaminating our food and the water we drink. Everyone then became infested with these evil parasites, causing the human race to suffer immeasurable pain and dissatisfaction. Had this been a prophetic dream meant to explain the state of the human condition? I recall the exact date that I saw the snakes from the rooftop: 1/19/11. When I Googled the date into my computer, I learned that 1-19-11 also happens to be the U.S. Pentagon's code for the Illuminati! Was the day of reckoning upon us? I was convinced that the end was near.

My paranoia was further intensified a few days later. I met a strung-out, red-headed kid outside of Rite Aid who was stumbling around, intoxicated on GHB in broad daylight. Since I empathized with him and did not want to see him accosted by the cops, I offered to escort him home. I paid for his subway ticket and together we traveled downtown, where he lived. He seemed very grateful for my help—that is, until we reached the block where he resided. Suddenly, he pulled out a hypodermic needle from his pocket, probably a lethal dosage of God-knows-what!

"I'm a member of the Bloods. You're on my turf now!" he said as he pointed the needle directly at me. He was referring, of course, to the street gang with which he was in alliance.

"Please tell me this is a joke. I have done nothing but try to help you today, and you are threatening to kill me?" Just then, a black woman appeared out of nowhere.

"What's going on here, honey?" she asked me. Just as I was about to fill her in, the red-headed kid scampered away. Clearly, God had sent me another one of his angels, just in the knick of time.

That same day, a friend of mine named Amanda stopped over. She was in hysterics. The "love of her life," her "soul-mate," had dumped her for another girl.

"You're not crazy, Daniel," she assured me. "Eddie is just like Jake. They are both shape-shifters, I swear!" Amanda, incidentally, had once tried to seduce Jake as well, and he turned her down flat. She was totally offended. "No guy has ever done that to me before," she insisted. "He *has* to be gay." Even I have to admit, Amanda *was* hot. I asked her if I could go down on her once, just because I was curious and she was right there next to me in nothing but her bra and underwear. "I'm on my period, sorry," she told me. I'm not sure whether she was just trying to turn me off or not. If so, it worked.

She wanted me to accompany her to Venice beach so she could get her belongings back from Eddie. When we got there, she ended up "throwing down" with Eddie's new girl in an alley way. I had never seen two girls fight like that before in my life. It was pretty scary, actually. They were rolling around on the ground like two wet wasps, pulling each other's hair, clawing at each other's faces, and punching and slapping each other profusely. And all of this commotion over some ugly-ass dude who cooked and sold meth. *Was it him they really wanted, or was it his stash?* I wondered. After a few minutes, the brawl ended when Amanda's ex-boyfriend punched her in the face, hard.

"You were cheating," he said. Cheating? I thought all was fair in love and war, no?

"I was kicking her ass!" said Amanda. "You had to break it up because she was losing, bigtime! See the way she's holding her hand in pain. She's obviously hurt, and I don't feel an ounce of pain right now."

"My hand is burning from punching your face so much," snapped the other chick.

"Your *soul* is burning," replied Amanda. Eddie then threatened to punch me in the face, just for being there!

"Please, don't," I said. If I had known that Amanda was going to drag me all the way to Venice Beach that day just to watch that horrific scene, I would have never gone in the first place! Thankfully, he backed off and moved away from me. People are completely ridiculous! The only reason to ever hit anybody is for self-defense. Period. That's the whole reason I wanted to apologize to my ex-boyfriend, Darrell, that day. I had acted like a total child when I tried to assault him in a jealous rage. I wanted him to know that I was sorry and that I had grown up a bit since then.

Neither one of us had any money to get back to Koreatown. But, once again, God sent us two new angels who drove us all the way home. It was at least an hour's drive with traffic. We met them at a gas station and there was an instant connection. They were a very attractive young couple, I must say.

"You're crazy pretty," I remember telling the girl, who went by "Coyote."

"Thank you!" she beamed. I then asked her if she knew that the earth was currently being invaded by aliens. "Of course," she smiled. "But the good people will be taken somewhere into outer space before things get really bad here. I am here to help those passengers board."

Before we parted ways, her boyfriend gave me a hug and said, "I'm glad I was able to help you with your journey." He then adorned my neck with a stylish string of rosary beads.

Was the rapture spoken of in the Bible about to occur? Would I be left behind?

Chapter 12

The Inquisition

Overly anxious and perplexed, I again needed a fix. I logged onto my usual website and began chatting with a local Asian man who lived just a few short blocks away from me. He invited me over to "party and play" (PnP, in the vernacular!), and he gave me the code to dial on the callbox when I arrived at his place. He instructed me to text him when I was nearby, which I neglected to do. Instead, I dialed his number on the callbox. It just rang and rang—no answer. I hung up and tried again, but I got the same results. Annoyed, I sent him a text that said, "OK???" Much to my surprise, he texted me back, asking if I was close-by. When I returned to his apartment complex a minute later and re-dialed the same number, this time he answered immediately and buzzed me into the building. Once I located his apartment, I stood quietly outside his door for a moment because I heard some commotion coming from inside. It clearly sounded like two people engaging in some sort of altercation. *Did I have the wrong apartment?* Then, quite suddenly, the commotion ended. It was now silent, so I knocked on the door.

He greeted me warmly with a smile. He was not wearing a shirt, and his body was stunningly chiseled, like a Greek statue. He was holding a glowing purple scepter in his hand.

"Is somebody else here?" I asked him. Sometimes, guys would invite me over and not tell me that it was a "group thing" until I was actually there. You gotta love surprises.

"No one but us," he responded. He then proceeded to show me around the apartment, all the while opening closet doors in order to prove that he wasn't lying to me.

"See," he said. "Nobody's in here, either!" It reminded me of a Looney Toons cartoon. ("He's not in here; he's *not* in here!" Then the proverbial bomb explodes as Yosemite Sam pushes Bugs Bunny aside and opens the closet door.) When I inquired about the purple scepter he was holding, he claimed it was a video game component, but I had never seen such a device before in my life. He also had an exquisite, hand-blown glass statue of Adam and Eve in his living room. There was a snake protruding from Eve's head, like a long ponytail. *Interesting*, I thought to myself. *We all have the same mother and she united with the snake, somehow.* After smoking meth from a bong, he exhaled the smoke into my mouth; it's called "shot-gunning," and I've heard it's a way to transfer more than just smoke. Thoughts, information, and power can supposedly be transferred that way as well. Just think about the way that God creates Adam in the Old Testament, by *breathing* his breath into the clay.

At this point, he began engaging me in conversation about my life and my thoughts. I mentioned my current fears of alien invasion and of being left behind after the rapture.

"Are you afraid to die?" he asked me.

"Not really," I responded. "After all, God has brought me this far. I think right now, I'm more afraid to *live*. I'm basically fed up with this world, and I don't feel like I belong here."

"Why do you seem so down?" he asked me. "You should remember to count your blessings."

"Believe me, I try, but there seem to be fewer and fewer to count these days."

"Remember that you will always have your youthfulness and your physical beauty," he reminded me. "Many people would trade their life's savings for those things, alone." And he was right. Every day I thank God for making me the lovely creature that I am. He then asked me about the tattoo on my right calf, which is a chain of turquoise rosary beads with an "M" dangling from them instead of a crucifix. "What does the 'M' stand for?" he asked me.

"It means "Music can be such a revelation," which is a Message from Madonna's Mouth." (The lyrics to the first verse of her classic dance song, *Into the Groove*.) "Music is the highest form of art," I continued. "It penetrates the soul. I see the universe as a giant record that plays a never-ending song. Each groove of the record represents every soul that exists—a collective, collaborative ensemble that creates a beautiful sound. It's all a matter of *finding* your *groove* in life and connecting to the natural rhythm of the universe. Music can be heard everywhere in nature. At the sub-atomic level, all things can be reduced to a musical note, a vibrational frequency. Music is like the blood of Christ, flowing through everything that *is*. Even in the Bible, God *speaks* the words, 'Let there be light,' which proves that sound came *before* light."

Very impressed with my answer, he put on a Madonna record and watched me dance, naked. Captivated, he lay back and admired my freedom as I surrendered to the sound. It was then that I realized that my relationship with God, though not sexual, can still be *erotic*. (Remember when Jesus bathes in the sea with his disciples?) Eroticism occurs when we are able to achieve a *balance* between excitement and relaxation, when we can be in motion and at rest simultaneously. This may seem like a contradiction, but as I mentioned before, life itself is a paradox—a beautiful mystery.

Every once in a while, I would catch him gazing mournfully up toward the heavens, as though he were praying for me. At on point, he went down on me briefly and then looked up at me and asked, "Do you still see me?"

"Of course," I replied. "Who else would I see?"

"I don't know," he answered. "I thought perhaps you saw the serpent." What a bizarre thing to say! Maybe, I thought, that the initial commotion I had heard before entering his apartment was the sound of another "guest" being devoured or strangled by the serpent. But since I had obviously passed the inquisition, I had escaped a similar fate and he did not transform into the snake this time. Had I seen the snake, I'm sure he would have used that scepter of his to send my body into oblivion, where it would have been overtaken by the next satanic lord who was waiting in line.

When I returned home, I Googled the word "Adeodatus," which was the screen name he was using online. As it turns out, that is the name given to the *Angel of Death,* who is sent by God to judge the wicked (in this case, people whose lives revolve around sex and drugs). Somehow, I had managed to charm the snake yet again.

Chapter 13

Nothing to Fear

"The only thing we have to fear is fear itself."
—FDR

Traumatized by my evening with the death angel, I stayed awake all night, fully expecting Jesus to descend from the heavens and separate the righteous from the wicked. Eventually, I fell asleep from exhaustion. When I woke up, I realized that I had slept through my shift at work. Impulsively, I called the restaurant and fabricated a lie about becoming violently ill on my way to work. I told my supervisor that I had forgotten to bring my phone with me on the bus, so I wasn't able to call until now. When I hung up the phone, I was disgusted with myself. I was always criticizing everyone else for lying, yet I had done the same thing out of *fear* of losing my job. As it turns out, they fired me, anyway. I got exactly what I deserved. I resolved not to worry about my own survival, though. Instead, I would trust in God to get me through somehow. I would let my soul provider be my sole provider.

Since I had absolutely no money, I decided to sell my mini refrigerator on craigslist. A pretty young blond girl responded to the ad. "Is it big enough to hold a bottle of wine?" she asked me. I told her that a wine bottle should fit nicely inside fridge's door. Then she asked me, "Is it clean, both the interior and the exterior?" I explained that it was in perfect condition both inside and out. It was only a few months old, after all. I made sure that it was shining like brand new when she came over to get it.

She had called me from a strange area code, so I decided to Google the area code. It just so happened that she was calling me from Oklahoma, and I had just read that very day that the Illuminati were the rumored culprits behind the infamous Oklahoma City bombing that took place in 1995. Was she another devil in disguise? When she arrived to pick up the fridge, she hastily told me that she had exactly *three* minutes to get in and out of the building since she had supposedly parked illegally. *Three minutes,* I thought, *is the usual detonation time of a bomb.* Had she been sent by the Illuminati to bomb the building where I lived in order to draw *blood from a stone?* While we were standing in my kitchen, her cell phone rang. She picked it up.

"Yes." There was a short pause as she allowed the person on the other end to speak. "Yes," she repeated. "Ok." Then she hung up the phone. Rushing as fast as I could, I handed her the fridge and she carried it down four flights of stairs.

"Could you open the gate for me?" she asked before she reached the stairwell.

"It's unlocked," I said, paranoid. "Have a good night." As soon as she was gone, I fled down the steps and out the door, my brow glistening with tiny sweat beads. I got as far away from the building as possible. I fully expected the building to explode. After about fifteen minutes or so, I started to realize just how silly I had been acting. I had been concerned only for myself—I had not even offered to carry the fridge for her, or even to suggest that she use the elevator instead of the stairs. It was then that I realized that—not only was she *not* a spy or a terrorist—but quite the opposite. She was yet another angel sent to me by God to help me realize that I was living in a state of *fear* and *selfishness.* And, as it says in the Bible, there is a place reserved in hell for the *fearful* as well as for all liars (Rev 21:8). Yes, this world may be very dark and dangerous sometimes, but God has armed his people with a shield of righteousness: "Yea, though I walk through the valley of the shadow of death, I shall fear no evil (Psalm 23:4)." It was then that I resolved to live and love *fearlessly.* The bottle of wine that she had inquired about clearly symbolized the blood of Christ, which cleanses us of our fears, sins, and frustrations. It affords us the opportunity to live eternally, without tasting death. Christ died so that we might live: "Take this and drink it, it is the blood of the new and ever-lasting covenant, shed for you (Luke 22:20)." When she asked me if the interior and exterior of the fridge were both clean, she was actually asking me about my body. The body is the temple of the Holy Spirit, so we are instructed to always keep it clean, inside and out. By using meth, I was not keeping my temple clean. And the "gate" to heaven, thanks to Jesus, *is* now unlocked.

Once I made the conscious *decision* to live fearlessly, the mysterious "pranksters" that had been invading my apartment suddenly disappeared. I no longer was seeing serpents, dragons, and reptiles everywhere I turned. Instead, I felt an abiding sense of peace, as though something *holy* now surrounded me, filling me with its serenity.

When I decided to sell my TV set a few days later, a man from the Philippines responded to my ad online. When he arrived to pick it up, I noticed that he was even smaller in stature than I am (and that doesn't happen very often!). I made sure to carry the television down the steps for him.

"Are you new to L.A.?" I asked him.

"Yes," he replied.

"Well, if you ever need anything at all, please don't hesitate to call me. This is a tough town, believe me, I know."

"I really appreciate that," he smiled. I then called a taxi for him from my cell phone and bought him a drink at the local market, which was next door to my building.

"Have a great night and thanks again," he said before getting into the cab.

* * *

Although Ron had technically been evicted from the building months ago, he was still living there, believe it or not. I remember visiting him one afternoon to tell him about my job termination. I was astonished to find him planting a rectangular field of topsoil and grass right there on his living room floor. It looked exactly like a gravesite. "What are you doing?" I asked him.

"Don't tell anyone, this is my own practical joke."

Practical joke? How could this possibly be construed as a "practical joke" if nobody was supposed to know about it? Clearly, Ron's mind was again being manipulated by the Unholy Spirit because it was weak and susceptible to invasion. He did not believe in God, plain and simple. In fact, he made it his personal mission to inform others that God did not exist!

"If you really believe there is a God, I'm here to tell you that there *isn't*," he said to me authoritatively.

"You're wrong, Ron." I said, shaking my head. "You don't have much time left to change your mind, either. Give yourself to Jesus, now."

"Well, bring Jesus over with you next time you visit," he joked. "If he's as cute as you are, I just *might* give myself to him."

I was not amused. It's strange, but a few months ago I would have been flattered by such a compliment from Ron. Now, it just sickened me. He was clearly drunk tonight on top of his usual valium-ephedrine cocktail.

"I'm feeling a little bit adventurous tonight," he said to me flirtatiously. "Why don't you spend the night here?" (Audrey, by the way, had long since moved out). I was dumbfounded. So *now* he was feeling "adventurous?" Now that he was staggering drunk and about to leave the building?

"I'll pass," I said in my bitchiest tone of voice. "Have a good night, Ron. Enjoy digging your own grave."

Chapter 14

Catch and Release

It killed me that everyone in the building labeled me as the "crazy tweaker," yet from my perspective it was everyone else who had seemingly lost their minds. I felt like the only sane person alive sometimes! Admittedly, I was still conflicted about my drug addiction, though. I was afraid that meth itself was becoming a false god to me. Yet, at the same time, I wanted to stay positive and optimistic, so I was willing to do whatever it took to maintain a level of hope—and meth made me feel more hopeful sometimes. I did intend to wean myself off it, eventually. I knew in my heart that Jesus really did not approve.

Like any good parent, God sometimes chastens or punishes his children as a form of loving discipline. In my case, this form of punishment presented itself on the day I was arrested for felony drug possession. I was on my way home one afternoon on the subway, which I often rode without paying the fare. Verification of payment was almost never required. On this particular day, however, there was a group of officers asking each passenger to show his or her ticket as they disembarked the train. Since I did not have a ticket and I was traveling with meth in my pocket, I panicked and tried to avert the officers. Noting my suspicious behavior, they searched me and found the meth in my pocket. Humorously enough, I had the meth stored in a pharmaceutical bottle labeled "Train Wreck" (which is a type of medical marijuana). After confiscating the contraband, two cocky policemen handcuffed me and drove me downtown to the jailhouse.

On the way there, I remember them asking me, "What are your fantasies?" *What an inappropriate and irrelevant question,* I thought. Once inside the jailhouse, they uncuffed me and asked me to stand against the wall, apparently so they could search me, again.

"My father's smarter than your father," one of the cops sneered at me. What was *that* supposed to mean? Were the police working for Satan as well? Did they intend to shoot me, execution-style, because I had told them in the squad car that I believed in Jesus? Once a "New World Order" is established under the rule of the antichrist, only those who have been branded with the mark of the beast will be able to work and survive within the system. The process of "weeding out" those individuals who refuse to cooperate with the New World Order has already begun. Many people will be put to death by the government for believing in Jesus Christ. Was I about to become a modern-day Christian martyr?

"Are you going to shoot me?"

"No. We're going to *rape* you. Now stand against the wall with your back facing us."

"Fuck no!" I yelled. "You just told me you were going to rape me!" They then tried to handcuff me again, but I miraculously avoided their attempt to do so, twisting my wrists around like Houdini.

"We're going to have to break your arms if you don't cooperate."

"Go for it," I said resolutely. Again, they tried their hardest to restrain me, but without success. Finally, they resorted to stripping me down to my bikini underwear (you didn't really think a princess would wear boxers, did you?) and wrapping heaving metal chains around my waist. Then they chained me to a metal bench which was inside a solitary confinement cell. There was a large window in the room, positioned so that everyone who passed by could see me. It was deliberately designed that way just to humiliate me. They left me chained there for over *ten* hours, with no food or water. I ended up pissing myself because I had no way of getting to the toilet. It was beyond inhumane. I started to think that maybe they were just going to leave me there to die of dehydration or starvation, so I began screaming for help at the top of my lungs—it was all I *could* do. Finally, just as my voice was about to give out, a female police officer heard my cries and came to my assistance.

"What are you doing down here, honey?" she asked me. I explained the entire situation to her, at which point she unchained me and escorted me upstairs.

"When do I get to see the judge?" I asked her.

"Probably in a day or two."

"Good," I replied. "Because when I meet with the judge, I am going to tell him *everything* that happened to me here. At the very least, I will have those two officers fired. And, if possible, I am going to sue this jailhouse and have you permanently shut down. There is absolutely *no* reason to treat a dog that way, much less a human being."

"Are you gay?" she asked me.

"Why does everybody keep asking me that question?" I said, annoyed.

"Well, you're definitely a hottie."

"Thanks, but flattery will get you nowhere right now."

I was then placed in a jail cell with three other men, all of whom were straight, of course. Everyone in jail is assigned a three-digit number by which they are known. Would you believe that my cellmate's prison number was 666? He was a twenty-six—year-old man who reminded me a *lot* of Jake in the way he acted. He kept softly chanting this creepy-ass song whenever he was around me: "I know I'm doing wrong, but I can't let you go . . . ." Those simple lyrics described my relationship with crystal meth in a nutshell! I knew I was not living the way God wanted me to, but I could not bring myself to stop using, either. Meth prevented me from giving myself to God fully. And as Jesus clearly states, "You are either for me or against me" (Matthew 12:30). There can be no middle ground.

"Are you gay?" asked #666. "You look like a mama's boy to me."

"I'm bi, I guess," I sighed. I was so tired of people asking me if I was gay. What difference did it make, anyway? "And I'm not a mama's boy. I'm Daddy's girl." By "Daddy," I was referring to God.

"You're bi, and they put you in *here*, with us?" he asked in disbelief.

It is California policy to keep the gay people in separate cells in order to protect them from harassment and/or abuse from other prisoners. I had no doubt in my mind that the officers had intentionally placed me in a straight unit, hoping that my cellmates would kill me so I wouldn't have the chance to tell the judge what they had done to me. But, as usual, nobody tried to harm me in any way. I stayed protected by the grace of God.

"Believe me," I assured #666. "I have less interest in having sex with you guys than you do in having sex with me." And that was the truth. I was not high for one thing, and none of them were at all attractive to me, anyway.

"Good," he said, after processing what I had just told him.

After three days in jail, they realized that my cellmates were no threat to me. So, the night before I was supposed to see the judge, they released me and dropped all the charges against me. It was as though the whole thing had never happened. Unbelievable. My brother had been caught with a comparable amount of heroin once, in the state of Georgia. He was placed on probation for *five* years, two of which he still has left to serve. Clearly, the cops were my worst enemy, but I did not want to pursue any charges against them. I was just thankful to be out of jail. I had my freedom back and that's all that mattered to me.

Chapter 15

Smile, Playboy, You're on TV

After being released from jail, I thought that perhaps I should just return to the East Coast to be with my family. After all, I had lost my job, I couldn't pay my rent (I had been served with eviction papers shortly after my three days in jail), and I was not exactly living a healthy lifestyle by anyone's standards. My days as a porn star seemed almost like child's play in comparison to the way I was living now.

Nicole was still living with her brother at this point, but she constantly complained that the two of them couldn't get along. I offered to let her take over my lease and move into my apartment so I could go back home. She enthusiastically accepted.

"I intend to stay here until the end of the month," I told her. "Please do not move any of your things into my apartment until I am gone."

"Don't worry, I won't," she assured me. Well, believe it or not, the very next morning she was pounding at my door, armed with knickknacks and suitcases full of her clothes. Wow, did this bitch have *nerve!*

"The deal's off," I yelled at her. "You clearly have no respect for me and you cannot be trusted."

Ron, who had *still* not left the building yet, overheard the commotion and barged in, attempting to somehow save the day again.

"The two of you are nothing but selfish, conniving *serpents!* I don't even want to look at your ugly-ass faces anymore!" I shouted at them. Nicole disappeared from my apartment, but she left all of her shit behind. I stormed downstairs to her brother's place. "Your sister is a *bitch!*" I explained what she had done.

"That sounds like Nicole," he said knowingly.

But as the weeks passed, I started to feel bad about the things I had said to her. (Why do I always have to be the better person?) So I apologized. "You're not ugly," I said to her. "You're beautiful; you know that. *I* was being ugly that day." I offered to take her to breakfast. I recall how rudely she treated the waiter that day, constantly bossing him around and complaining about the food. When we finished eating, she suggested that we go grocery shopping at the supermarket directly across the street from the restaurant. As a courtesy, the supermarket offered a transportation van that drove people home who did not have their own vehicles. While waiting for the van to arrive in the hot sun, I removed my t-shirt. I was wearing a tight black tank top underneath it. Just as I took my t-shirt off, a young talent agent approached me. He was grocery shopping with his wife and their newborn baby. They had just moved to L.A. from Texas a few weeks beforehand.

"I'm only 24-years-old, but I'm the second biggest agent in the adult industry," he bragged. *Good for you,* I thought to myself facetiously.

"Would you be interested in working for Playboy TV? I'm currently casting and I think you would look great on camera." Nicole, who was busy loading the back of the van with her groceries, overheard our conversation. Before I could even answer him, she practically pushed me out of the way.

"Are you looking for girls? I'm a model and I'm always looking for work. I have tons of experience in front of the camera."

"I'm looking for both guys and girls. I'm sure I could use both of you."

We exchanged phone numbers and went our separate ways. A few days later, he called us both and asked if we'd be interested in doing a scantily clad volleyball scene together on Playboy TV. He also had another gig lined up for Nicole which involved some sort of ridiculous "Penis Olympics." Her job would be to manually use various penises as slingshots by placing peanuts on them and then trying to aim the peanuts toward a bucket. The Penis Olympics game was scheduled to be shot the day before the volleyball scene, and we would be paid in cash upfront for both. It just so happed that the day of Nicole's shoot was the *last* day that the landlord was able to accept rent money from me in order to have the eviction process reversed. Nicole would be making exactly what I needed, so I asked her if I could borrow the money from her for *one* day.

"If you lend me the money you make at your shoot, I can pay my rent. Then, when we do the volleyball scene together the next day, I will directly hand you my earnings and we will be squared away." Would you believe that she refused to spot me the money for *one* day? I had let her stay with me, rent free, several times and had never asked her for a cent or pressured her to move out. She didn't even *need* the money, really. Her brother wasn't charging her any rent, and she was receiving $200 a month in food stamps. Every time I allowed her back into my life, she would do something to once again fall from my graces. She ran downstairs in tears. I followed her, livid.

"I'm the one who hooked you up with that agent in the first place! If it weren't for me, you wouldn't even *have* the job!" I shouted.

"Well, it was *my* idea to go to the grocery store where we met him," she said.

"Maybe so," I countered, "But the only reason we were at the store at that time was because I took you out to breakfast. It always comes back to me, doesn't it, Nicole? I'm always going to be one step ahead of you! I'm always going to be smarter than you, and I'm always going to be prettier than you!" As I spoke these abrasive words, her brother's roommate took it upon himself to interrupt me.

"Get out of my apartment," he ordered me.

"*Your* apartment? Nicole's brother lives here, too, and he invited me in. So shut the fuck up, this doesn't concern you." Well, that *really* set him off. He charged toward me and physically assaulted me, pushing me up against the wall and calling me a "crazy fuck."

"You attack me over something that has *nothing* to do with you, and yet I'm the crazy one?" Personally, I think he was just another closeted homo who was secretly in love with Nicole's brother. He had this tattoo on his arm that read "Girls Are Evil" and I often felt a jealous vibe from him whenever I was over there. Nicole's brother and I often got into some pretty intense conversations, and he probably felt left out. Besides, Nicole's brother was damn sexy. "The truth hurts, doesn't it, bitches?" I screamed at Nicole and her brother's roommate as I slammed the door behind me. This time, I promised myself, I was done with Nicole for good.

A few days later, I received a phone call from the casting agent's wife. Apparently, Nicole had seduced him in order to obtain more work. She must have done a great job of it, too, because he abandoned his wife and newborn son to be with Nicole (and he had known her for less than a week!).

"I need you to give me whatever dirt you have on Nicole," his wife said, "because there may be a custody issue when we go to divorce court."

"I'm very sorry to hear about this," I consoled her. My heart genuinely hurt for her. "Unfortunately, I don't have much information to give you. Nicole is certainly not a *moral* person—OK, that's an understatement. The whore of Babylon has *nothing* on Nicole. But I am not aware of any legal trouble or violations that she has committed. Sure, she smokes a lot of weed, but that's legal here in California." As much as I wanted to put Nicole in her place, I could not possibly bring myself to bear false witness against her. To make matters worse, Nicole and her new beau rented a unit together on the third floor of the building where I lived. And, now that they were an item, any opportunities I may have had with him as far as casting went down the tubes.

Since I was no longer working and my social life was stagnant, I decided to audition for a play in North Hollywood. It was called *The Boy with Three Balls,* a mature comedy about a young man who lived in a building with a bunch of crazy assholes who constantly harassed him, yet they all thought that *he* was the crazy one. Talk about metatheatre! I swear, the part was written for me. I hadn't done much acting in recent years, but in high school and college I was very much involved in theatre and highly respected, locally, as an actor. I showed up at the audition completely unprepared. I had no headshot and no resume, but I managed to land the *lead role.* I suspect that the director cast me because the role required full nudity in several of the scenes—and he was an older gay man who gave the eye as soon as I walked in the door. Why was it, I wondered, that the only jobs I seemed to qualify for were the ones that involved removing my clothes? Surely, I had to serve some other purpose in this world besides driving men wild with lust! Unfortunately, the show was cancelled early because half of the cast ended up backing out at the last minute. To be honest, I wasn't all that disappointed about it because I really wasn't looking forward to prancing around on stage, butt-naked, in front of an auditorium full of fully-dressed strangers. Besides, the show was scheduled to be performed twelve times without a written contract guaranteeing me a set amount of money. A pretty shady deal, all things considered.

I was also cast in a music video for a song called *Problem Child*. They were looking for eccentric people who were unafraid to "be themselves." At first, I thought I was a perfect fit for this. But I soon realized that they were looking for outlandish "freaks" such as drag-queens and overly-tattooed/pierced people who try a little *too* hard to stand out. I'm sorry, but clothes do *not* make the man. What someone wears cannot begin to express who that person *is*. I remember meeting a guy in a gay club once who was wearing a very large, very tacky cowboy hat.

"What's with the cowboy hat?" I asked him.

"It's who I *am*," he answered me indignantly. At the time, I was wearing a gray skull cap, which I promptly removed from my head.

"You see this?" I asked him. "This is *not* who I am. It's my fucking *hat*."

Another acquaintance of mine, who lived in my building, had promised to cast me in a commercial that he was supposedly shooting in San Francisco. I was so excited about the opportunity and the trip to the City, yet that deal fell through, as well. It was as though everyone around me was trying to build me up just so they could tear me back down again! I was quickly getting fed up with all the bullshit—the "California snow," if you will. So, I decided to just indulge in more California *ice*.

Chapter 16

Vanity is Insanity

A man by the name of Jeff, whom I'd met online a few months ago, offered to come and pick me up so we could party together. Although I was not really into him, how could I say no to free drugs? As soon as I saw him, I noticed a definite change in his appearance. His eyes, which had once been kind and gentle, were now cold and icy. *Great,* I thought, *another victim of demonic possession.*

I distinctly remembered the religious debate he and I had gotten into the first time we had met. Although he had been raised in a Christian family, he had since renounced his faith in Jesus because the Bible did not condone the lifestyle of sexual debauchery that he was living. Religion and the church had left him feeling inadequate and "unworthy," he had told me. The reality is that we all fall short of God's glory. The only way to become purified is by accepting Christ into your heart. You then become one with His spirit and your sins are wiped away.

"What have you been up to?" I asked him.

"Oh, just fucking around," he replied smugly. I'm sure this was a jab at me and the way I had been spending my time since being fired a few months ago. "Is this the same building you lived in last time?"

"Yes, don't' you remember driving me home that day?"

"I do remember dropping you off, but I was coming from the *other side* at that time." The implication, of course, was that he had been traveling from the other side of town, except that that explanation made no sense at all, since he still lived in the same place (Hollywood) and we had taken the very same route to my building. I know for a fact that he came to pick me up directly from his place. What he actually meant by "the other side" was that on our first encounter, he had been a human being. He was now a satanic lord.

By this time, however, I was convinced that God would protect me regardless of the situation I put myself in, so I got in his car and we headed toward Hollywood. Once we arrived at his apartment, he suddenly began lecturing me about my sense of "entitlement." Was I developing a reputation among the online tweakers in L.A.? Was I rumored to be a drug-seeker who used people only for their drugs? While this may have been somewhat accurate, I didn't feel guilty about it because I never pretended to befriend anyone or care about them on a deeper level. In fact, I seldom saw the same guy more than once. I never bothered anyone. If they wanted to call me for a repeat performance, that was their choice. Besides, they were using me for *sex*, so what was the difference? Wasn't that a fair exchange? Admittedly, I usually tried to get away with doing the least amount of "work," sexually, as possible (unless I happened to be really into the other guy, which didn't happen very often).

By "entitlement," it's also possible that he may have been referring to my lack of interest in finding another job. Sure, I had filled out a few applications and gone on a couple of interviews, but I was unwilling to do any type of work that would bring me down or break my spirit. I considered that to be no better than prostitution—selling myself out in exchange for money. After all, God would find a way to keep me alive, right?

I glanced over at his computer screen. As his background, he had the famous Andy Warhol painting of Marilyn Monroe in the colored squares. Only it wasn't Marilyn's face inside the boxes, it was his own face. Or, rather, it was the face of the Jeff I had met the first time. The portraits of Jeff were displayed in a museum, with people looking up at him, as though his former self obtained immortality only through those paintings. The *real* Jeff was dead and gone. I was particularly struck by the computer background because—that very afternoon—Arnie had given me a poster that featured the faces of Madonna, Charlie Chaplain, Andy Warhol, and Albert Einstein. Einstein was holding up a picket sign that read "Love is the Answer." It took me a while to figure out what these four icons had in common, but then it hit me: Love is such a simple concept, yet nobody seems to really get it! It takes a genius (like Einstein, Warhol, Madonna, or Chaplain) to grasp such a simple idea. I had also noticed that, drawn inside Andy Warhol's forehead on the poster, was a blurry image of my very own face. When I pointed it out to Arnie, he exclaimed, "I do see it!"

It was then that I decided that—like Marilyn Monroe—I was a true work of art, the brainchild of the greatest artist and chief musician of all. After all, we as humans do not really *create* art ourselves—it is simply transmitted through us from a higher power. "I want that Warhol template," I told Jeff. "I want to put my own picture in place of Marilyn Monroe's."

"I can copy the template to a disk for you," he offered.

"Cool," I said. "I just had a bunch of professional photos taken of myself. Maybe you can help me choose the perfect one for the Warhol design." I logged onto my email account, where I had set up a slide show of my pictures so I could share them with my friends. When I opened up the slide show, however, I was unpleasantly startled by what I saw. The pictures that I had been so pleased with had been altered somehow. In every single one of them, my face was completely scarred up, as though I had been through a fire! "Why does my face look like that?" I stammered aloud.

Jeff ignored the question. He just sat there, pretending to read a magazine. Just then, another man—a complete stranger—walked into the room.

"I'm Mitch. I've heard about you, Daniel."

"How's it going, Mitch?"

"I'm doing OK. I just got back from Palm Springs. There were a lot of bitter, resentful people there with nasty attitudes. They all had this sense of *entitlement* about them, as if the world owed them something. And it was very *hot*." As he said the word "hot," he lighted up a torch lighter. I suddenly realized that these two tweakers had brought me there with the intention of torching up my face with the lighter, which is why my face was scarred in the pictures. It had been a premonition—a warning of what was about to transpire. I immediately stood up.

"I'm going to go now," I said nervously.

"How will you get home?" Jeff asked, surprised.

"I'll figure it out." As quickly as I could, I bolted out the door and ran down the street. I had no idea how I was going to get back home, since I had absolutely no money and it was about 4:00 a.m.

As I reached for my cell phone to check the time, I realized that I had inadvertently left it at Jeff's place! I had left in a panic. I was so disoriented by this point that I couldn't even find my way back to his apartment. All the buildings looked the same to me, and I didn't know his address. Should I just forget about the phone? I walked underneath a bridge, where I was confronted face-to-face with a skunk. *Great,* I thought, *this is all I need right now.* I stood there, motionless, the skunk staring directly back at me. A moment later, it scampered away. Just then, another angel appeared out of nowhere. He was wearing a black blazer and sported a goatee.

"What's wrong?" he asked me. I explained the situation to him—how I had left someone's house because I didn't trust him, but that I had accidentally left my phone behind.

"What's his name?" he asked me.

"Jeff."

"There's nobody named Jeff on this street." How could he know that? Did he know the name of every person who lived on the street? There were hundreds of apartments there! The stranger let me use his phone to call my own phone. Sure enough, Jeff picked up. He agreed to meet me at the nearby 7-11 so he could return the phone. (Oh, and the stranger was right—I *was* on the wrong street!)

"Would you mind coming with me?" I asked him.

"It's a brightly lit intersection. You'll be fine. The problem has been solved."

I thanked him and walked toward the 7-11. When Jeff pulled up, he handed me my phone.

"I'm sorry," he said.

"For what, exactly?"

"For everything that happened tonight."

"You didn't do anything," I muttered. (Although I'm sure he had plans to do something!) Was this a lesson meant to teach me not to get too caught up in my own vanity?

"Have a good night." He nodded and drove away. When I got back home, I immediately checked my email and looked at the pictures. They were back to normal again.

The very next day, while I was waiting for the train to arrive at the subway station, I noticed a beautifully groomed brown Pomeranian. Since I am a huge dog-lover, I moved closer toward it to get a better look. "What a beautiful dog!" I said to the owner, whose back was facing me at the time.

"Oh, thank you!" she replied in a sweet, gentle voice. As I looked up at her, I was instantly taken aback by her mutilated face. Either she had some sort of disease, or she had been in an explosion. Either way, every inch of her complexion was completely covered in giant, purple boils, her features unrecognizable. She made Freddy Crougar look like Freddy Prince, Jr. (I wish that were an exaggeration.) I did everything in my power to disguise the look of shock that I know must have been on my face. There were several other people there waiting for the train, all of whom were unable to stop staring at her.

"He's been such a blessing to me," she continued.

"I have a dog, too, and he's always been my best friend." She seemed so well-adjusted to her condition, and I really had to admire her for that. As I was exiting the train station, I approached another passenger whom I had seen speaking to the same woman. He had completely ignored her appearance and had treated her with dignity and respect.

"Let me ask you something," I said to him. "If you woke up one morning and you looked in the mirror and saw something like *that* staring back at you, could you ever really be happy again?"

"Of course," he said.

"I'm not sure I could," I confessed. "My personal philosophy has always been "Stay sexy and fuck all else!"

"Well then, you're happy, right?"

I thought about this for a while. Was I happy, really? I mean, sure, I was able to look in the mirror and feel satisfied with my physical reflection. But if I were *truly* happy, then why would I still need to be using meth? Maybe it was time to re-think my personal philosophy.

Chapter 17

Love is the Answer

The next day, as I was alone in my apartment getting stoned and listening to the radio, the song *Father Figure* by George Michael came on the radio. When I heard the lyric, "*When you remember the ones who have lied, said that they cared but then laughed as you cried . . . . beautiful darling, don't think of me, because all I ever wanted is in your eyes . . . .*" I instantly thought of Nicole and it moved me to tears. I realized that I had been unforgiving toward her. Sure, she had treated me unfairly, but in the grand scheme of things, all arguments (especially about money) are petty. If I could not forgive her for the way she had treated me, how could I expect God to forgive me for my own transgressions? Still crying, I ran downstairs and burst through her door without knocking.

"What are you doing here?" she said, startled. "You aren't welcome in my home!"

"Baby, please, just give me five minutes! I just want to apologize for the things I said to you. We *have* to stop this fighting." Her new boyfriend ushered me outside onto the fire escape.

"What are you on?" he asked me.

"Nothing, except for weed, I swear."

"Don't lie to me. You wouldn't be shaking like that unless you were on something."

"I'm shaking because Nicole has me a nervous wreck! The landlord may have evicted me from the building, but she has evicted me from my *life!*" Just then, Nicole joined us on the fire escape.

"Dinner's ready," she told him. "Come inside and eat."

"Just give me a few minutes with Daniel," he replied. I had suspected ever since our first meeting at the grocery store that he had a secret gay crush on me. Even now, he preferred to be on the balcony with me, instead of inside with her. *It has a dick,* I thought to myself, *of course it wants me.*

"You know I would have done anything within my power to help you when you needed anything," I said to Nicole. "But you are never willing to return the gesture toward me."

"I have shared food with you many times." *Big deal,* I thought. *She doesn't even pay for it, the government does.*

"Man cannot live by bread alone, baby," I reminded her.

"Actually, they did it once, in Israel," said her new beau.

"He's good," I said, smiling. "I have to admit it, he is good!"

"Fine, we're not fighting anymore," Nicole said while rolling those gorgeous brown eyes of hers. Once again, things were at peace, for the time being, at least.

A week or so later, Nicole came to my door, sobbing. "My boyfriend cheated on me!"

"And this surprises you, how?" I said while lifting up my right eyebrow. After all, he had left his wife and kid for Nicole after knowing her for only a week! And he was a porn agent, for God's sake! Was she really expecting long-term monogamy here? It was then that I realized just *how* foolish some women can really be.

* * *

Even though I was penniless and facing eviction, I decided to just not worry about myself. I met an old man on the street who approached me, saying, "My friend, can you spare any money at all? Anything from a penny to a million dollars will do. Obviously, a penny is low and a million dollars is too high, but someplace in the middle will do nicely."

"I'm sorry," I told him. "I really wish I could, but I am broke myself."

"Don't worry about money, my friend," he told me. "You have a good heart. There are more important things in life than money." And he was absolutely right.

So I began to focus on humanity. I was convinced that my primary responsibility in life was to be a guardian angel, to go out and spread the word of God to anyone who would listen to me. "The Titanic is about to sink!" I warned people metaphorically. "I hope you know how to walk on water!" The story of the Titanic is, of course, a prime example of the ego self-destructing. Those who built the ship were pompous and overly proud of their work; they were sure that even God himself could not destroy it.

I dubbed myself "Adam Michael: Captain of the Federation of Light." (I borrowed the name "Adam" from the book of Genesis and "Michael" from the Archangel Michael.) I built an altar in my apartment out of a bamboo tree which I prayed at, daily. Surrounded by candles and burning incense, I knelt there and prayed for humanity. Once you learn how to love *unconditionally*, other people's pain and suffering become your own pain, just as Jesus suffered on the cross by taking the sins of others upon himself. I thought of Jake, a lot. "Daddy, I love him!" I would cry. "Please heal him." I even sent a text to Jake which read, "Your mind and those arms of yours will be forever *weak* until you learn to use them to embrace me." His response was a vague "OK." God is always there with open arms, just waiting to take us under his wing. As individuals, we must decide whether we will welcome his embrace or deny his existence by choosing to serve our egos instead.

Crystal meth, after all, had been invented as a war weapon during the Second World War to help increase productivity and to keep the Axis powers focused on the task at hand. I chose to use it for my own weapon in a spiritual battle. I failed to acknowledge at the time, however, that the Axis powers *lost* the war and they were also completely evil! If I did not stop using meth, it would ultimately destroy me. But, like any addict, I was in denial. I used any excuse I could muster to justify my habit. Eventually, even Tim stopped talking to me completely. Stubbornly, I told him that "Jesus Christ is my savior and He is the only friend I need."

"You're wrong," Tim responded. "*Tina* Christ is your savior." ("Tina" is a common slang word for meth.)

Since I was being faced with the possibility of eviction and I've never been materialistic, I offered Boss, who lived across the hall, anything he wanted from my apartment. "You are welcome to anything except for my *Love is the Answer* poster," I told him. "It has sentimental and personal value to me." I left my door unlocked and ventured back out to do more "light work." When I returned home, I was shocked to find that my poster had been taken down. Angrily, I knocked on Boss' door. He opened it.

"What's up?" he asked innocently.

"I told you specifically *not* to take that poster and yet it's gone. Why would you do that? Were you intentionally trying to upset me?" I expected him to apologize or tell me that he had done it as a practical joke. Instead, he reacted defensively.

"Don't come at me like that," he barked. "You can have your damn poster back. You're lucky that I'm giving it to you when I oughta beat your ass." I was astounded.

"This can't be happening. This can't be real. I thought you were my friend?"

"Just take your stupid poster and get the fuck out." I was truly hurt by this. I had been more than generous by offering him anything he wanted, except for that poster, free of charge. And he deliberately defied me. What an asshole! Prior to that incident, I had had nothing but respect for him. The next day, just to prove I was the better person, I taped the poster to his front door, hoping he would read the words "Love is the Answer" and understand that message. There is never a need for fighting or making threats to bodily harm someone else, especially a friend. The right thing for him to do would have been to return the poster and apologize for his behavior. Instead, he kept it. Boss and I barely spoke again after that.

Chapter 18

Sweet Dream or Beautiful Nightmare?

> *ALIEN PRINCESS: A woman who acts as if the normal rules of being a human on planet Earth do not apply to her. She conducts her life in this manner with an attitude of entitlement that she should be treated differently and well, lavished upon even, but reciprocation is not necessary on her part. She is convinced this is the way to live her life, even though her experience is that good decisions in another galaxy are simply bad decisions here on planet Earth.*
> —Urban Dictionary, defined June 21, 2011.

A few days later, I befriended a lovely woman named Cassie in the building. She, too, liked to "party" often, but she was beautiful, inside and out. She lived with a 65 year-old man named Bob, who supplied her with the drug and she would generously share it with me daily. One time, Bob stormed out of his apartment and threatened to bash my face in because I had overheard the two of them arguing inside their apartment. Cassie had told me that he was frequently physically abusive toward her. I tried to intervene by pounding on the door and threatening to call the police. Outraged, he swung the door open and narrowed in on me.

"Stay the fuck away from us or I'll fucking kill you!"

"You're just jealous because you're ugly and I'm beautiful!" I snapped. I believe that inner ugliness inevitably leads to outer ugliness. Clearly, he was both.

Cassie thanked me repeatedly, referring to me as her "handsome savior." So of course, I let her move in with me for as long as she wanted to be there. I could not bear the thought of her living with Bob and subjecting herself to any further abuse or degradation. I was surprised to discover that Cassie was actually my long-lost alien twin sister! She, too, identified as an alien princess, and we had both been exiled to the same tower, apparently.

"If you feel like you're under constant surveillance, you're not paranoid," she told me. "And even if you *are* a little bit paranoid, that still doesn't mean that you aren't being watched." She went on to explain that she and I were actually celebrity superstars in some other dimension. The cameras were perpetually rolling, filming our lives in a reality show for the entertainment of millions in an alien galaxy somewhere. Our cell phones had tracking devices planted in them so that our whereabouts could be determined at any time, she told me. "It can be a little bit unnerving because they just don't respect our privacy the way they did in the old days," Cassie told me. "And the government knows all about it, too, so don't let them fool you. They're all in on it. That's why it's so hard for us to land any other roles in other projects. We're both stuck in the same goddamn contract." That certainly explained why all of my recent employment endeavors had mysteriously fallen through! And, while it was kind of cool to know that the aliens found me to be *that* fascinating, I still cannot pick my nose or wipe my ass without feeling overly self-conscious about the whole thing.

One day, Cassie and I were out doing our job as light-workers (I had to recruit my own sister, after all!) and we passed by a hotel. I'm not sure why, but something compelled me to go inside and approach the front desk.

"Can I help you?" asked the clerk.

"Yes. I stayed here once, a few months ago." This was true; I had spent the night there with a Brazilian drug dealer who had a huge crush on me at the time. "I've since noticed that my crucifix has been missing. It's a silver cross with the body of Jesus on it, on a silver chain." Now, I *had* lost my cross, but it was not a crucifix and I had only lost it a few days ago. The clerk proceeded to open a drawer and pull out a silver crucifix on a silver chain, exactly as I had described. He handed it to me. I thanked him and walked out the door, amazed. I placed the crucifix around my neck, along with the round silver metal I wore. Whenever anyone asked me why I wore the silver medal, I would say, "Because I plan to finish in second place. Not bad, right?" The implication, of course, is that Jesus wears the gold!

* * *

Although my eviction papers had mandated that I leave my apartment by March 15, 2011, it was now the end of May and I was still there. I hadn't paid rent since January, mind you. I was still convinced that God would keep me there as the "Guardian of the West Gate." Even the landlord didn't seem to mind my being there at all. "I fully intend to pay you what I owe as soon as I am able to," I explained. "I have no doubt that I am going to be very successful one day soon."

"Well, if nothing else, at least you still have a dream," he said. What a powerful statement! Even if everything is your life seems bleak, the most important thing is to keep *believing* that things can turn around in an instant. I, for one, was still a believer.

That is, until the police came knocking on my door one morning, forcing me out of my apartment. I could hardly believe it! I honestly thought that I would be able to live there, rent free, forever! Obviously, I was suffering from drug-induced delusions. They gave me fifteen minutes to pack up whatever I could carry and then they escorted me out the door and changed the locks. They did not, however, order me to leave the building itself. So I simply took my belongings upstairs and put them in an empty room that had been vacant ever since I had lived there. I figured I could just stay there until I could find other arrangements. I slept on the hard wood floor with no blankets or pillows, but at least I had running water and electricity. I scanned my list of contacts in my phone, but there was nobody that I felt comfortable calling for assistance. I had met and slept with dozens of men during the past year in L.A., yet I hadn't made one single friend. Sad. I stayed in the vacant room for about a week or so, until one day the landlord intercepted me.

"Speak of the devil," he said. "You're not allowed in the building anymore. You are considered to be a liability and you've already cost us nearly 5,000 dollars in unpaid rent." Honestly, I hadn't really cost them anything. There were several unoccupied units; it's not like I was preventing a paying tenant from moving in.

"But I thought you were OK with my being here? I thought we had talked about this? I am still the same person I was a week ago, before the police came."

"It doesn't matter. Come back on Monday and we can set up an appointment for you to retrieve your belongings."

"Monday is not a good day for me."

"Why not? You don't do anything. You don't work. The party's over, dude."

"No, it's not," I laughed.

"It is, in this building. Now leave before I have to call the police."

I had no choice but to turn and walk away, since I certainly didn't want to deal with the police again. In truth, Monday was not a good day for me, though. I had been cast in a commercial for a line of unisex cosmetics (I guess that role was actually suitable for an alien princess!). I dreamed of becoming the first male "Cover Girl." I was certain that the spirit of Anna Nicole Smith was watching over me. I had spent so many nights mourning the tragic, untimely death of Anna Nicole and her son, Daniel. (She had also named her daughter Dannielynn, so there was an obvious spiritual connection between us.) Anna Nicole, like myself, was another Marilyn—the real deal. She was a kind-hearted person who had been misjudged as a gold-digger and persecuted by the media. The money was obviously not of paramount importance to her. It was the death of her son that destroyed her. At his funeral, she tried to crawl inside his coffin with him, insisting that she did not want to live if he had to die. "Daniel, you were my rock, and why God took you away from me, I'll never know," she said. Even now, I cannot think about Anna Nicole without breaking into tears.

I lived on the streets for a few days. Then, on Monday when I arrived at the photo shoot, I felt the powerful presence of Anna Nicole. I introduced myself to another one the models. "My name's Daniel Fritz," I said. "But I'm sure it translates to Anna Nicole Smith in some language."

"Absolutely," she smiled. "And my name's *Danielle,* so your name is easy for me to remember." As I stood on the rooftop that day, surrounded by beautiful men and women, I felt incredibly blessed. The photographer had me stand in the center of a ring of models with my eyes focused toward the sky. As I gazed toward the heavens, I read the word "SUPERIOR," which was written in giant letters on a nearby skyscraper.

The photo shoot's location was only a block away from my former home on 7th street. Directly after the shoot, I went to a local internet café and logged onto my usual website. Maybe I just wanted to prolong the natural high I had experienced at the photo shoot? In any event, I found myself heading toward the home of yet another stranger who promised to get me high. When I arrived there, he had very little meth to share, but he had about a gallon of GHB. He instructed me to "gulp it down," which I foolishly did. You think I would have learned my lesson about GHB after being mugged on Santa Monica Blvd. But at the end of the day, an addict is still an addict! Within minutes, I was a total wreck. Aggravated with my messy behavior and constant chattering, he threw me out while I was still intoxicated.

It was about midnight, and my plan was to go to Tim's place, hoping he'd forgive me and take me in for a while. (Tim lived only a few blocks from where I was at the time.) I had to piss really badly, so I decided to relieve myself right there on the street behind a parked car. While I was in mid-stream, would you believe that a police officer appeared directly behind me? Fuck my luck! I was still highly intoxicated from the GHB; I could barely see straight.

"Who are you?" I asked, paranoid.

"Santa Monica Police Department." There was another officer with him and they were both beyond irate. "He's fucked up on something!" They searched me, then forcefully bent my arms back and handcuffed me, violently forcing me into the back of the squad car. When we arrived at the police station, things got much worse. They threw me on the cold cement floor, both of them mounting my back while pushing my face into the floor. My chin-length hair was conveniently draped over my face in order to hide my facial hair, so they could "pretend" I was a girl, I'm sure. (I was wearing a pair of girl's jeans, size 3, and a tight white tank top.) Clearly, they were playing out their sadistic rape fantasies in their own heads—it was a crime against *women*. They bruised my breastbone, which took a month to heal completely.

"You are nothing but goddamn, mother-fucking PIGS!" I screamed at them, repeatedly. There was a female cop there, who was watching the entire scene. She seemed shocked by the whole thing, but was too afraid to intervene on my behalf. They locked me in a private cell, where I vomited all over the floor. "Let me out, please!" I begged. The male cops simply scoffed and mocked me in a whiny tone of voice.

"Let me out, pleeeese," they taunted me. Eventually, I calmed down and realized that I wasn't going anywhere. I started doing some stretching exercises.

"Are those Pilates or yoga?" asked the female cop. "That's good for the *heart*."

They eventually moved me into a holding cell with two other prisoners. One of them was clearly schizophrenic, and he kept belligerently threatening to kick our asses. The other prisoner yelled out "He's trying to hit us!" at which point the cops came barreling through the door to restrain him. They moved him into another cell.

"Do you want to press charges against him?" the cops asked the other guy. I found this question to be utterly hysterical. He had not so much as laid a *finger* on either of us, but they wanted to prosecute him. Yet the police themselves had brutalized me and bruised my breastbone? Unreal!

"It's too bad that all cops go to hell," I said to my cellmate. "It's not really fair to the ones who are just trying to support their families."

I will admit that there was one officer who treated me nicely. Later that day, I was placed in a holding cell with all the straight guys, at which point he beckoned me outside the cell and asked me if I was gay. When I told him that I didn't really mind being in with the straight guys, he said, "Sometimes people can act stupid, though. I just want to make sure you're safe." I thanked him. If only he had known how "stupid" the police were capable of acting!

I spent the night in jail and the next day the judge gave me "time served" as a sentence. If she had only known what I'd been through during that one night, she probably would have given me a complementary cruise to Hawaii! I was not allowed to speak on my own behalf, and the public defender did her best to have the "public urination" charges dropped. She told me I would have to write a "letter of complaint" about the Santa Monica Police department if I wanted to pursue brutality charges against them. I recall seeing some graffiti on the cell wall that read "Fuck SMPD." *That's right,* I thought. *Fuck 'em. Let them have their fun now. They'll get what they deserve, eventually.*

Chapter 19

Full Circle

"Oh, what a tangled web we weave when we practice first to deceive."

—*Sir Walter Scott*

After I was released from jail, I went to Tim's place and pleaded my case to him. "I'm sorry I was so hard on you before," I told him sheepishly. "It turns out that I really *do* need you as a friend, and it was wrong of me to put you in the same category with all the other men who have used me for sex in the past. And you were right, I have to stop using meth immediately or it will destroy me. I know you care about me, but my drug problem is just too much for anyone to handle."

"You haven't been making the best decisions since you moved out here, but I will always be your friend, regardless," he told me. Finally, someone who actually understood what it means to love unconditionally!

We both agreed that I should get on a plane and go back to my parents' house in Georgia before I got myself into any more trouble. After all, enough was enough. I wasn't even sure I was enjoying the drugs anymore. I remember the Death Angel had told me, "Once it stops being fun, it's time to quit using." He had also advised me not to ever do GHB again, and I hadn't listened, resulting in extremely painful repercussions. It was time to stop testing fate.

I knew that returning home to my family wouldn't exactly be easy, either. I did not feel welcome there by my father, who had never really approved of my sexual orientation. He considered himself a "failure" because he had raised a gay son. When I arrived at my parents' house, my mother was in Pennsylvania visiting my sister, so my father lashed out at me. He told me I was nothing but a problem to him, that I was "ruining his life" and "no longer his son." Then he started belittling me about my past career as a porn star, calling me a "pervert."

"I'm sorry I didn't turn out to be straight," I told him. "But a parent's love, like God's love, is supposed to be *unconditional.*" My father had been verbally and sometimes physically abusive to me as a child, and my siblings and I had never quite gotten over the emotional scars. "I'll tell you what," I said to him. "I won't use the past against you anymore if you promise to stop using the past against me."

He paused for a moment, and then said, "You got a deal, buddy." He shook my hand and, for the first time *ever* in my lifetime, I saw a glimpse of a *real* person; I saw into his soul. *Maybe there is hope for humanity after all,* I thought.

I logged onto my Facebook page and discovered that Jake had accepted my recent friend request on there. He sent me a message explaining that he, too, had stopped using meth. He asked me if I still lived on 7th Street. As usual, he was trying to find someplace to stay. I'm sure he did not want to return to *that* building, though, because he had more than worn out his welcome there and didn't want to deal with Boss again. When I told him that I had moved out of that apartment, he told me to text him. "It's Grant," he said.

Wow, this kid had *balls!* After everything that had happened between us, he was *still* trying to take advantage of my soft spot for Grant. I also noticed that, on his Facebook page, he had written in his profile that, "I'm straight. I don't mess with other dudes, that's gross." Didn't he realize that publicly asserting his heterosexuality just made him look that much more insecure about it? He also posted that he was "tired of being single" and that a "girlfriend would be nice; it's too bad I'm not around anyone right now." Not around anyone? You live in L.A., the second most populous city in the U.S.A., for Christ's sake! Just admit you like guys! His image (what *other* people think of him) is obviously too important to him for that to probably ever happen. Although he may not be a reptile from below the earth's soil, he will remain ungrounded until he can accept his true self. Until he comes to terms with his sexuality, Jake will remain one of the millions of antichrists who live in the world today. These people live a lie and serve their own egos, the *antithesis* of their true, God-intended selves. Sad.

"I hear Miley Cyrus is still single," I commented.

It's funny, but now that I have been through rehab and I'm sober, I fully understand that Jake, Nicole, and Ron were all manipulative, conniving users who probably cared nothing about me. They just took advantage of the fact that I was lonely and desperate. But I was the one who *allowed* them to, so it's nobody's fault but my own in the end. I also understand that, once you are *truly* grounded, that is the time you become *accountable* for your own actions. You can no longer use the excuse that the "devil made me do it."

A lot of people avoid relationships because they are afraid of being hurt, or taken advantage of, or because they just want to avoid the drama. But here's the deal: sometimes all of those things are necessary because they help you to eventually figure out what love is *not*. Even evil has its place in the end.

In ancient mythology, life is compared to a labyrinth. In order to find the goddess who lives in the center of the maze, you have to follow *one* path. Everyone has the same lessons to learn in life in order to free their inner goddess. Some of us have to learn the hard way, but sometimes the hard way is the only way to really learn! Once you free the chained-up little girl inside, you surrender to the reality that God is in control and that he will never abandon you. You can finally stop depending on other people for your own sense of self-worth. There is no longer a need to be afraid of who you are, or to be unhappy or discontent with your current circumstances. It doesn't matter how difficult things may seem, either. When you are at your lowest point, it is pretty much a guarantee that things are going to improve; the tide is about to turn. The key is to trust in God, always. Once you can do that, you are finally free to be what you were created to be—an incarnation of unconditional love. And you must maintain that sense of hope and confidence *without* the help of drugs, because if it isn't *real*, then it isn't right.

If you have a substance abuse problem, I am not going to preach to you and tell you that you have to stop using this very second. I certainly would not have listened to anybody a year ago if they had told me to stop using. And believe me, many people tried. When you're ready, you will stop. Try to stay strong, though, because if I can overcome, so can you.

Each of us has been blessed with our own unique gifts in life, and we all have a story to tell. When our stories are shared openly and honestly—without fear of judgment—they become much more valuable. I have always been a gifted writer, and I have known my entire life that someday I would write a book. I just had to wait for the right timing and the right inspiration. For me, the time is *now*, so I decided to share *my* story with you, in writing. What you choose to do with my story is entirely up to you. I remember seeing a CD in a record store in L.A. entitled *Wasting Light*. By not using our God-given gifts to connect with other people, we allow our inner light to be wasted. Those who do not use their gifts will eventually have their talents and their inner light taken away from them. Thank you for giving me the opportunity to share one of my gifts with you!

Yes, I still consider myself to be the Alien Princess, and I'm still living in a tower that's guarded by a dragon. But I am no longer *trapped* there! I am just waiting for the day when I will receive my promised inheritance. And, unlike most human beings, God *always* keeps his promises.

So what's the next step in my life? Well, now that I can say—with confidence—that I love myself, I am ready and able to find someone else who understands how to love him/her self, and together we can co-create something endlessly beautiful. But, should that not happen, I am perfectly fine with staying single—and celibate—for the rest of my life, too. I am a lonely soul no more! As most recovering addicts will tell you, hitting "rock bottom" often allows you to transform from a caterpillar into a butterfly. During my downward spiral in L.A., I may have lost "everything" in the material sense, but I still managed to hang onto my own soul—which is really the only thing I ever needed in the first place! With this realization, I am finally able to leave my lonely cocoon and take flight. At last, I am free to love fearlessly, selflessly, and unconditionally.

Now that I am clean and sober, I think my next move may be to New York City. A friend of mine, who has also struggled with crystal meth, lives there. He worries that New York City may not be the best place for me right now, since meth is highly prevalent there. If my experiences in L.A. have taught me anything at all, though, it is that I cannot keep running from my own personal demons; I have to face them head-on. I now understand that *temperance*, or moderation in all things, is the key to healthy living. Crystal meth and other hard drugs are not meant to be taken in moderation, nor is it really possible to just do them socially. It is time to leave meth where it belongs—in the past.

I think I can handle the "Big Apple," now that I've tasted the "forbidden fruit" in Los Angeles. Is the Alien Princes ready for New York City? I think the more appropriate question is: "Is New York City ready for the Alien Princess?" Stay tuned. I will definitely keep you posted! Peace and love.

CPSIA information can be obtained at www.ICGtesting.com
Printed in the USA
LVOW06*1519061213

364187LV00002B/49/P